BEST OF Dinosaur Jr.

2   Almost Ready

15 Feel the Pain

20 Forget the Swan

35 Freak Scene

43 Little Fury Things

52 Not You Again

63 Out There

78 Raisans

87 Sludgefeast

97 Start Choppin

109 Thumb

116 The Wagon

Music transcriptions by Aurélien Budynek

ISBN 978-1-4234-6985-8

HAL•LEONARD® CORPORATION
7777 W. BLUEMOUND RD. P.O. BOX 13819 MILWAUKEE, WI 53213

For all works contained herein:
Unauthorized copying, arranging, adapting, recording, Internet posting, public performance,
or other distribution of the printed music in this publication is an infringement of copyright.
Infringers are liable under the law.

Visit Hal Leonard Online at
www.halleonard.com

from *Beyond*
Almost Ready
Words and Music by J Mascis

C G D C
let ring
End Rhy. Fig. 2
Gtr. 3: w/ Rhy. Fig. 2
G D C G D
Gtr. 1
P.M.
Gtr. 2
let ring
C G D C
let ring

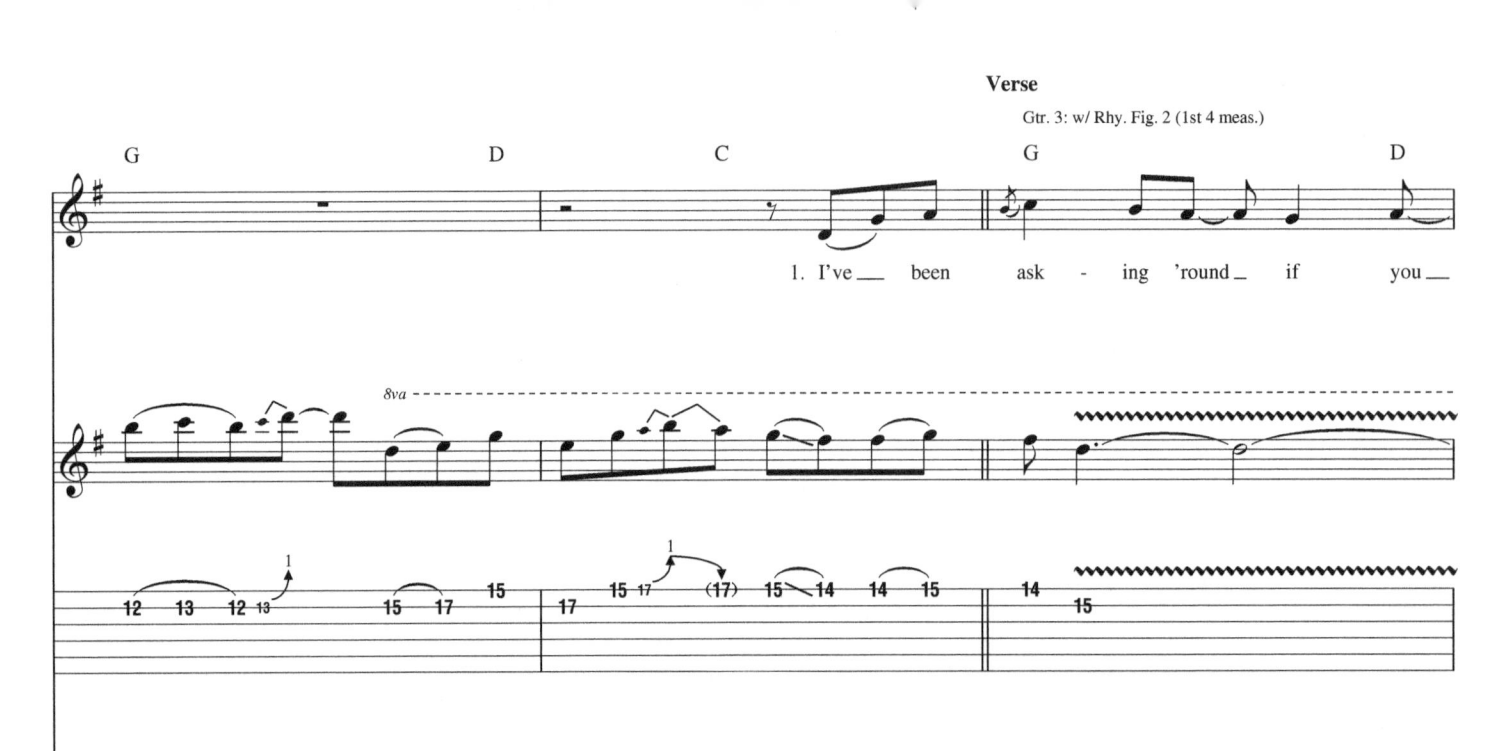

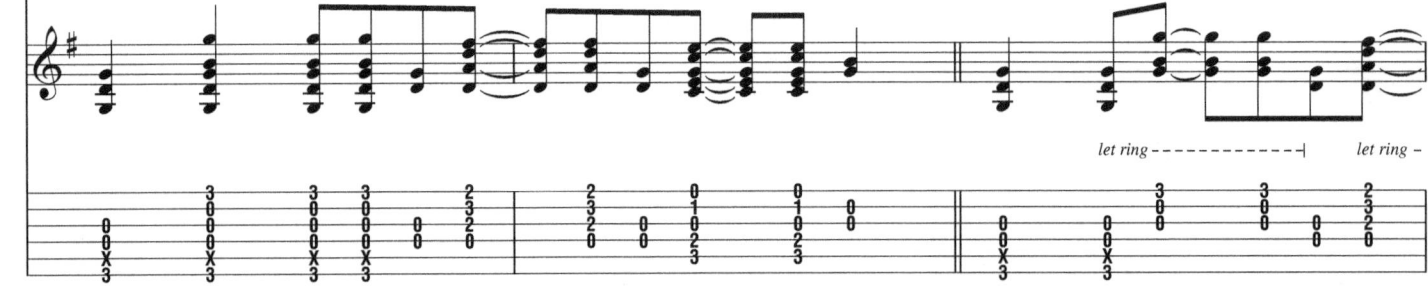

Verse

1. I've been asking 'round if you were there. Asking, but I'm always scared.

G D C G D C N.C.
Ask - ing 'cause I want to care a - gain. Come on,
Gtr. 4 (dist.)
mf
Gtrs. 5 & 6 (fuzz)
Fill 1
End Fill 1
f
P.M.
Gtr. 2
Rhy. Fill 1
End Rhy. Fill 1
let ring
let ring
let ring
P.M.
Gtr. 3
Rhy. Fill 1A
End Rhy. Fill 1A
P.M.

Chorus
1st time, Gtr. 4 tacet
G D C G D C
life, I'm al - most read - y. Not
Gtr. 6
Riff A1
End Riff A1
Riff B1
End Riff B1
P.M.
let ring
Gtr. 5
Riff A
End Riff A
Riff B
End Riff B
P.M.
Gtr. 3
Rhy. Fig. 3
P.M.
let ring
Gtr. 3
Rhy. Fig. 3A
P.M.

To Coda
G D C G D C
right,
al - most read - y.
I'm al - most read - y.
I'm al - most read - y.
2. I've been
3. Can you
let ring
Fill 2
End Fill 2
End Rhy. Fig. 3
End Rhy. Fig. 3A

Verse

Gtr. 2: w/ Rhy. Fig. 1 (3 times)
Gtr. 3 w/ Rhy. Fig. 2 (1st 6 meas.)
Gtrs. 5 & 6 tacet

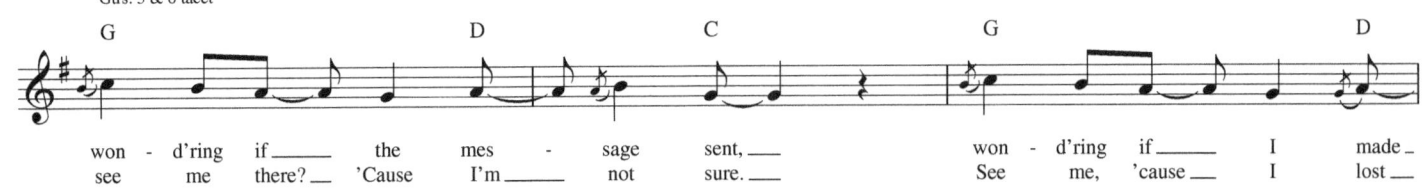

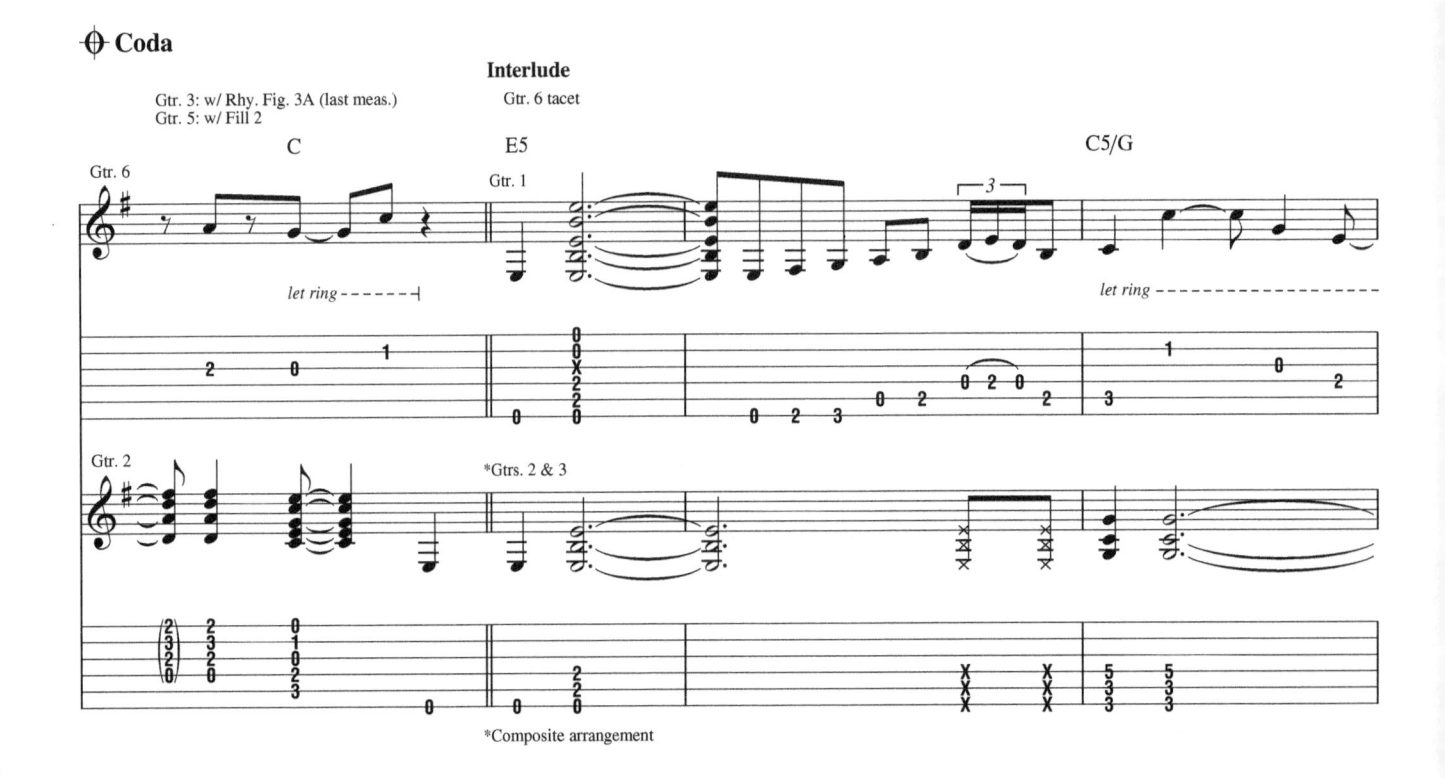

won - d'ring if____ the mes - sage sent,__ won - d'ring if____ I made__
see me there? 'Cause I'm____ not sure.__ See me, 'cause__ I lost__

__ a dent,__ won - d'ring what__ it is____ you meant__ a - gain.__
__ my nerve.__ See me there,__ 'cause I____ feel worse__ a - gain.

D.S. al Coda

1.
Gtr. 3: w/ Rhy. Fill 1A   Gtrs. 5 & 6: w/ Fill 1

2.
Gtr. 3: w/ Rhy. Fill 1A   Gtrs. 5 & 6: w/ Fill 1

Come on,____   Come on,

Coda

Interlude

Gtr. 3: w/ Rhy. Fig. 3A (last meas.)   Gtr. 6 tacet
Gtr. 5: w/ Fill 2

*Gtrs. 2 & 3

*Composite arrangement

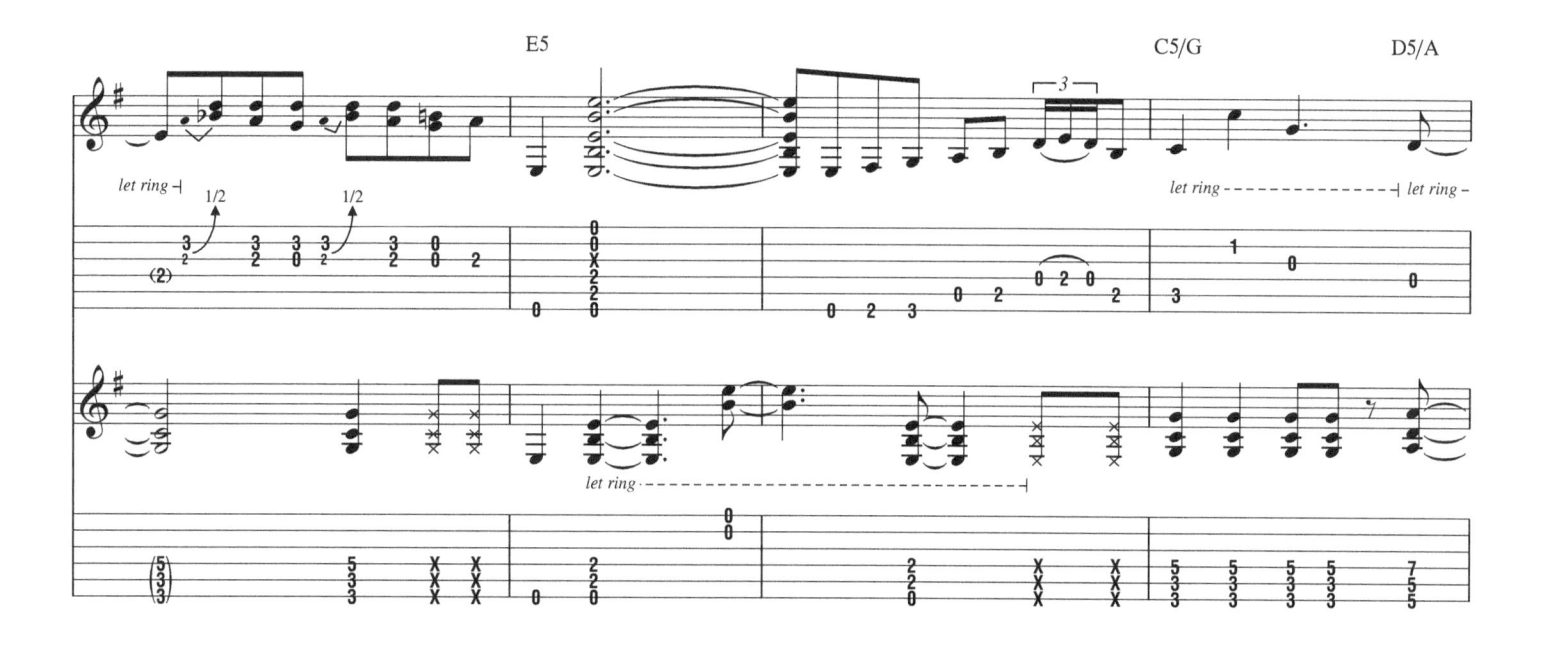

Verse

4. Let me find the truth, __ I will __ at - tack. __

Find the truth, __ I won't __ go back. __ Find the truth, __ I'm way __

C G D C
off track a - gain.
let ring
let ring
let ring
let ring
Guitar Solo
Gtr. 2: w/ Rhy. Fig. 1 (3 times)
Gtr. 3: w/ Rhy. Fig. 2 (1st 6 meas.)
G D C G D
Gtr. 7 (fuzz)
8va
loco
C G D C
Gtrs. 2 & 3: w/ Rhy. Fills 1 & 1A
Outro-Chorus
Gtrs. 2 & 3: w/ Rhy. Figs. 3 & 3A (1st 6 meas.)
Gtrs. 5 & 6: w/ Riffs A & A1
G D C N.C. G D
Come on, life,
Gtr. 7
grad. bend
Gtrs. 5 & 6
P.M.

Gtrs. 5 & 6: w/ Riffs B & B1 (1 1/2 times)
C G D C G D
I'm al - most read - y. Not right,
Gtr. 7
Gtrs. 2 & 3: w/ Rhy. Fills 1 & 1A
C G D C N.C.
I'm al - most read - y. Come on,
Gtr. 7
Gtr. 8 (fuzz)
Gtr. 6
let ring
P.M.
Gtr. 5
P.M.

Gtrs. 2 & 3: w/ Rhy. Figs. 3 & 3A
Gtrs. 5 & 6: w/ Riffs A & A1
Gtrs. 5 & 6: w/ Riffs B & B1 (7 times)
G D C G D
life,
I'm al - most read - y.
Gtr. 7
hold bend
hold bend
Gtr. 8
C G D C
Not right,
I'm al -

Gtrs. 2 & 3: w/ Rhy. Figs. 3 & 3A (last 2 meas., 2 times)
G D C G D
- most read - y.
Al - most read - y.
C G D C
Al - most read - y.

14

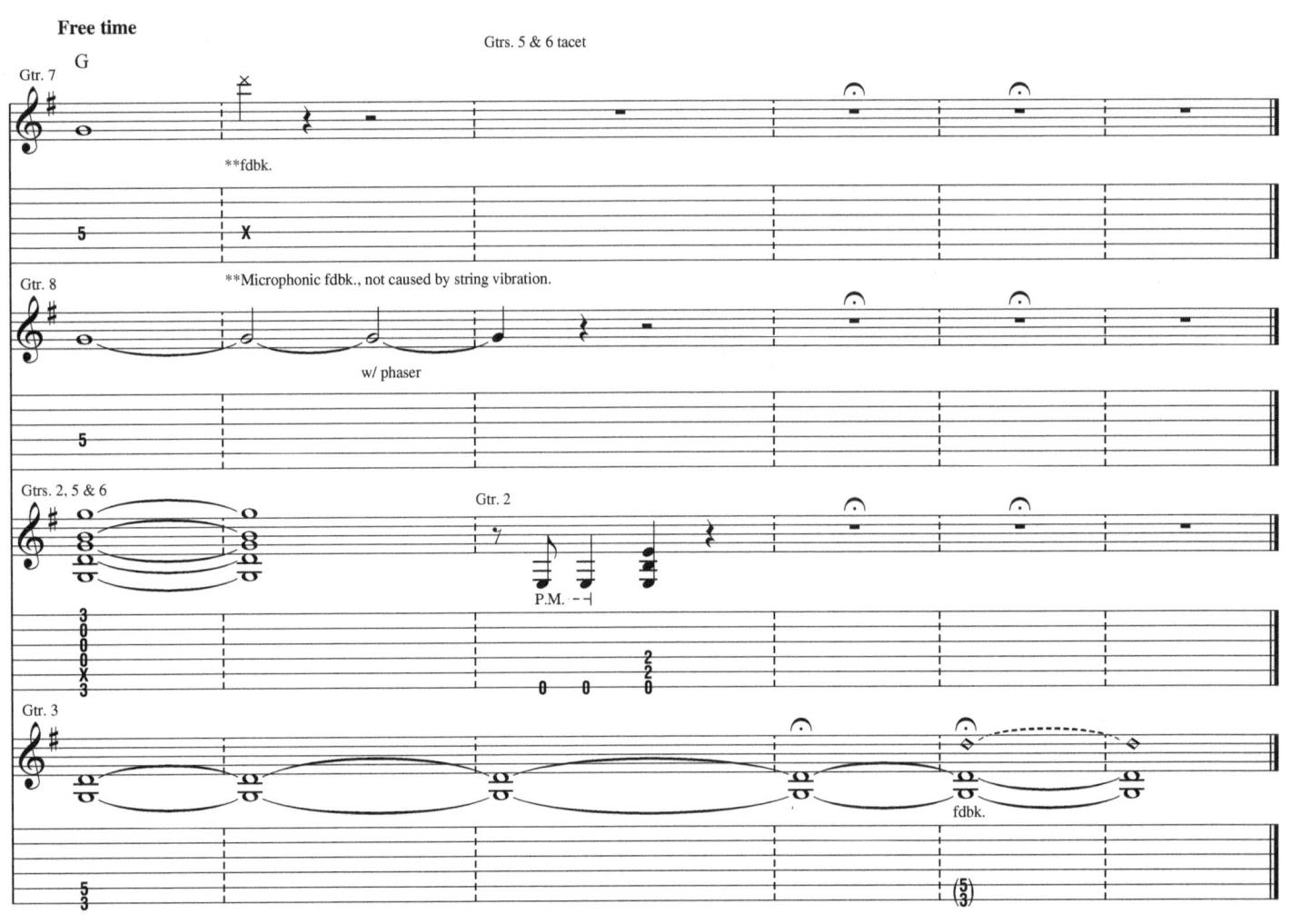

from *Without a Sound*

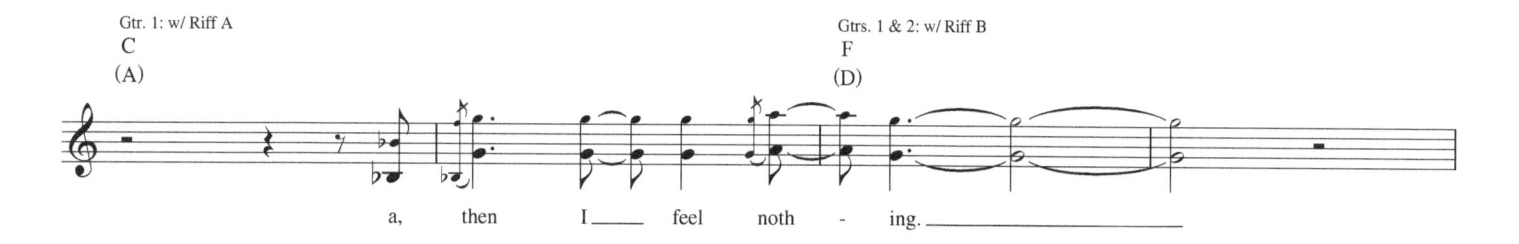

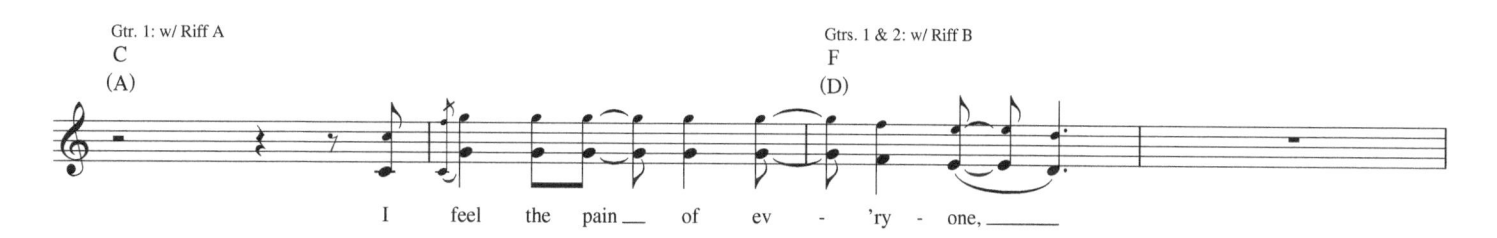

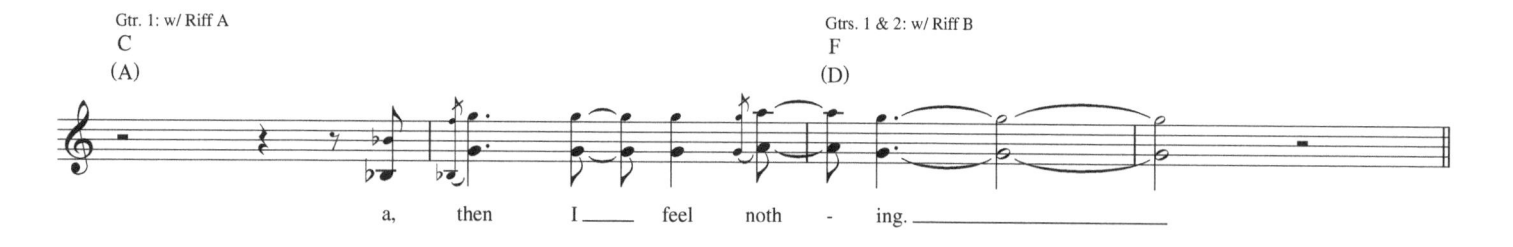

Feel the Pain
Words and Music by J Mascis

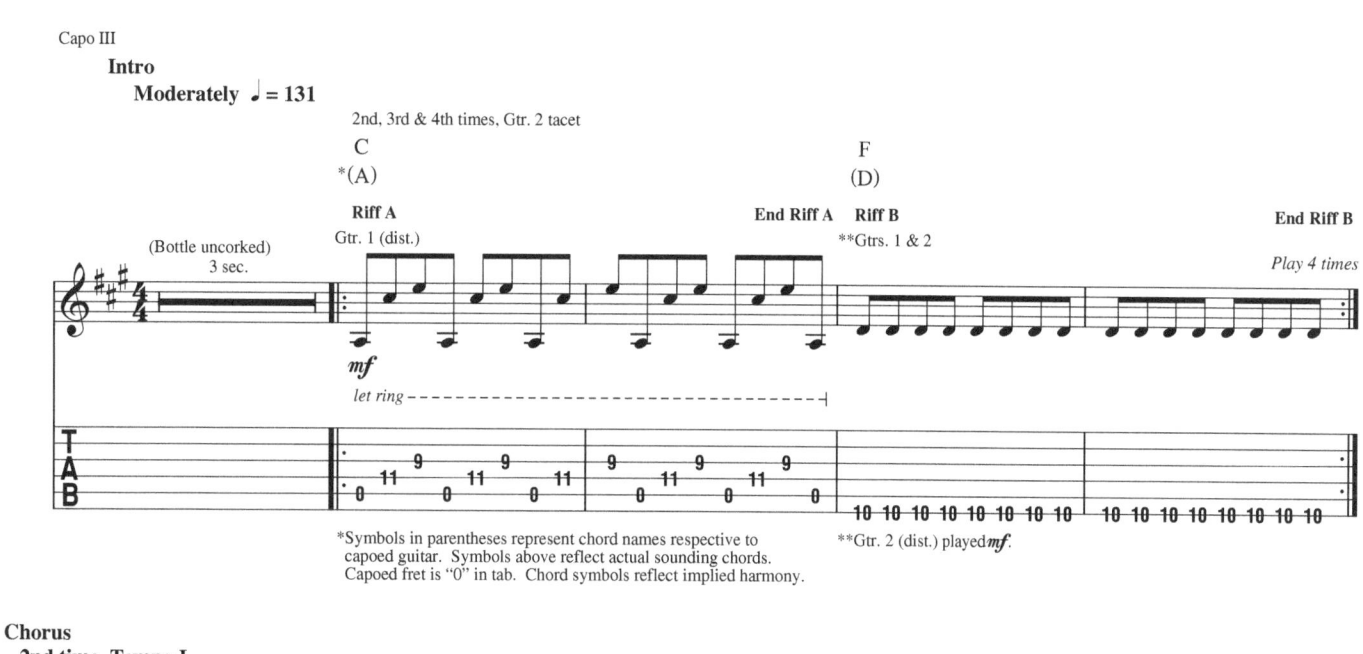

Capo III

Intro
Moderately ♩ = 131

2nd, 3rd & 4th times, Gtr. 2 tacet

C   F
*(A)   (D)

Riff A   End Riff A   Riff B   End Riff B
Gtr. 1 (dist.)   **Gtrs. 1 & 2   Play 4 times

(Bottle uncorked) 3 sec.

mf
let ring

**Gtr. 2 (dist.) played *mf*.

*Symbols in parentheses represent chord names respective to capoed guitar. Symbols above reflect actual sounding chords. Capoed fret is "0" in tab. Chord symbols reflect implied harmony.

Chorus
2nd time, Tempo I

Gtr. 1: w/ Riff A   Gtrs. 1 & 2: w/ Riff B
C   F
(A)   (D)

I feel the pain of ev-'ry-one,

Gtr. 1: w/ Riff A   Gtrs. 1 & 2: w/ Riff B
C   F
(A)   (D)

a, then I feel noth-ing.

Gtr. 1: w/ Riff A   Gtrs. 1 & 2: w/ Riff B
C   F
(A)   (D)

I feel the pain of ev-'ry-one,

Gtr. 1: w/ Riff A   Gtrs. 1 & 2: w/ Riff B
C   F
(A)   (D)

a, then I feel noth-ing.

Copyright © 1994 Spam As The Bread Music
All Rights Administered by Chrysalis Songs
All Rights Reserved Used by Permission

Interlude
Faster ♩ = 152
C (A)
F (D)
C (A)
F (D)
Riff C
*Gtrs. 1 & 2
End Riff C
*Composite arrangement
Gtrs. 1 & 2: w/ Riff C
C (A)
F (D)
C (A)
F (D)
Bridge
Faster ♩ = 162
Dm (Bm)
G (E)
Gsus4 (Esus4)
Is it up to me?
Gtrs. 1 & 2
Rhy. Fig. 1
Em/B (C♯m/G♯)
Fmaj7/C (Dmaj7/A)
Am (F♯m)
G (E)
You won't wait to see.
End Rhy. Fig. 1
Em (C♯m)
Screwed us {both / yet} a - gain.
let ring
let ring

'Bout as close as you've been.

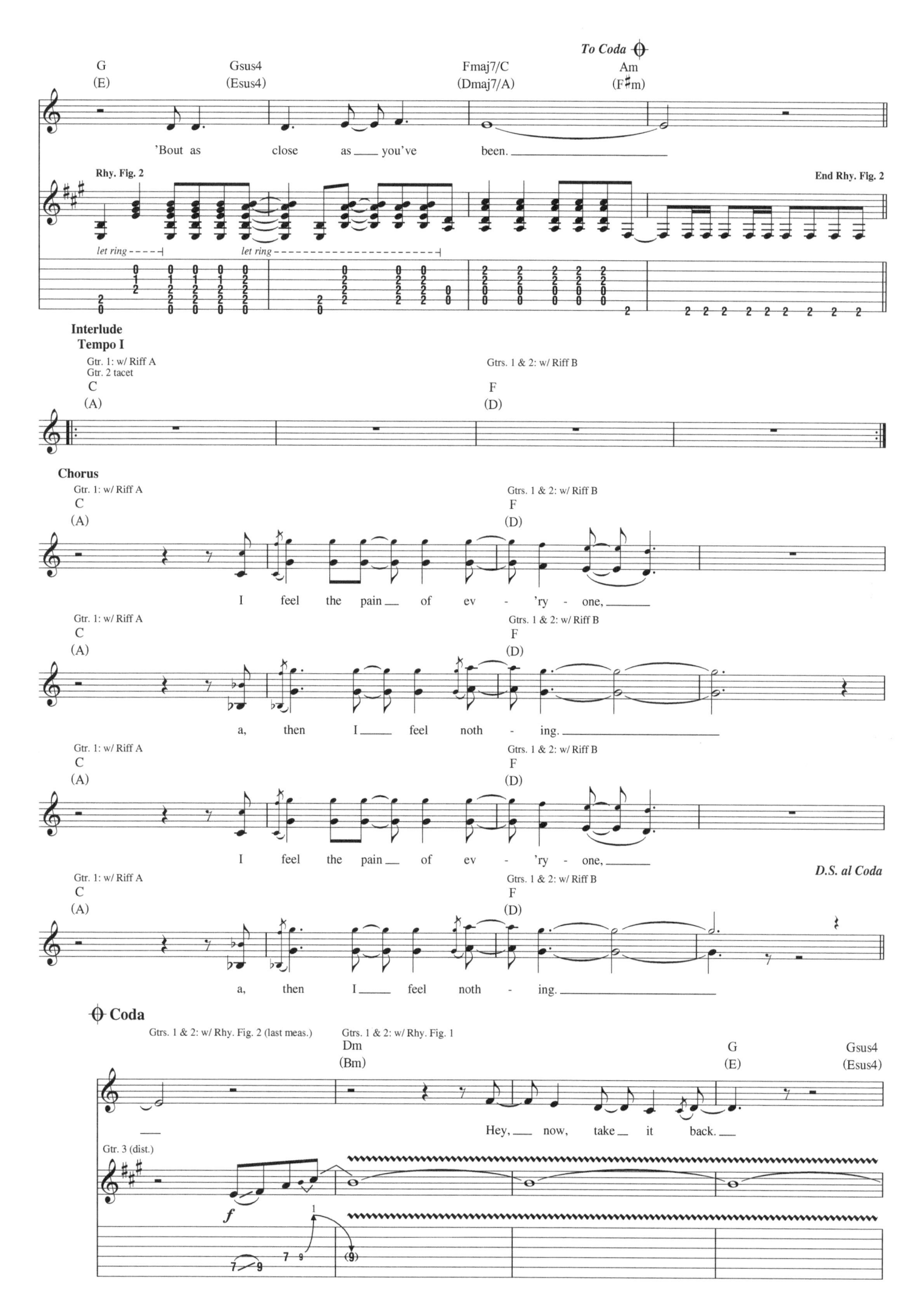

Interlude
Tempo I

Chorus

I feel the pain of ev - 'ry - one,

a, then I feel noth - ing.

I feel the pain of ev - 'ry - one,

D.S. al Coda

a, then I feel noth - ing.

Coda

Hey, now, take it back.

17

Lyrics:
Get off the attack.

Trailing on your scene.

Just try and keep it clean.

Outro-Guitar Solo

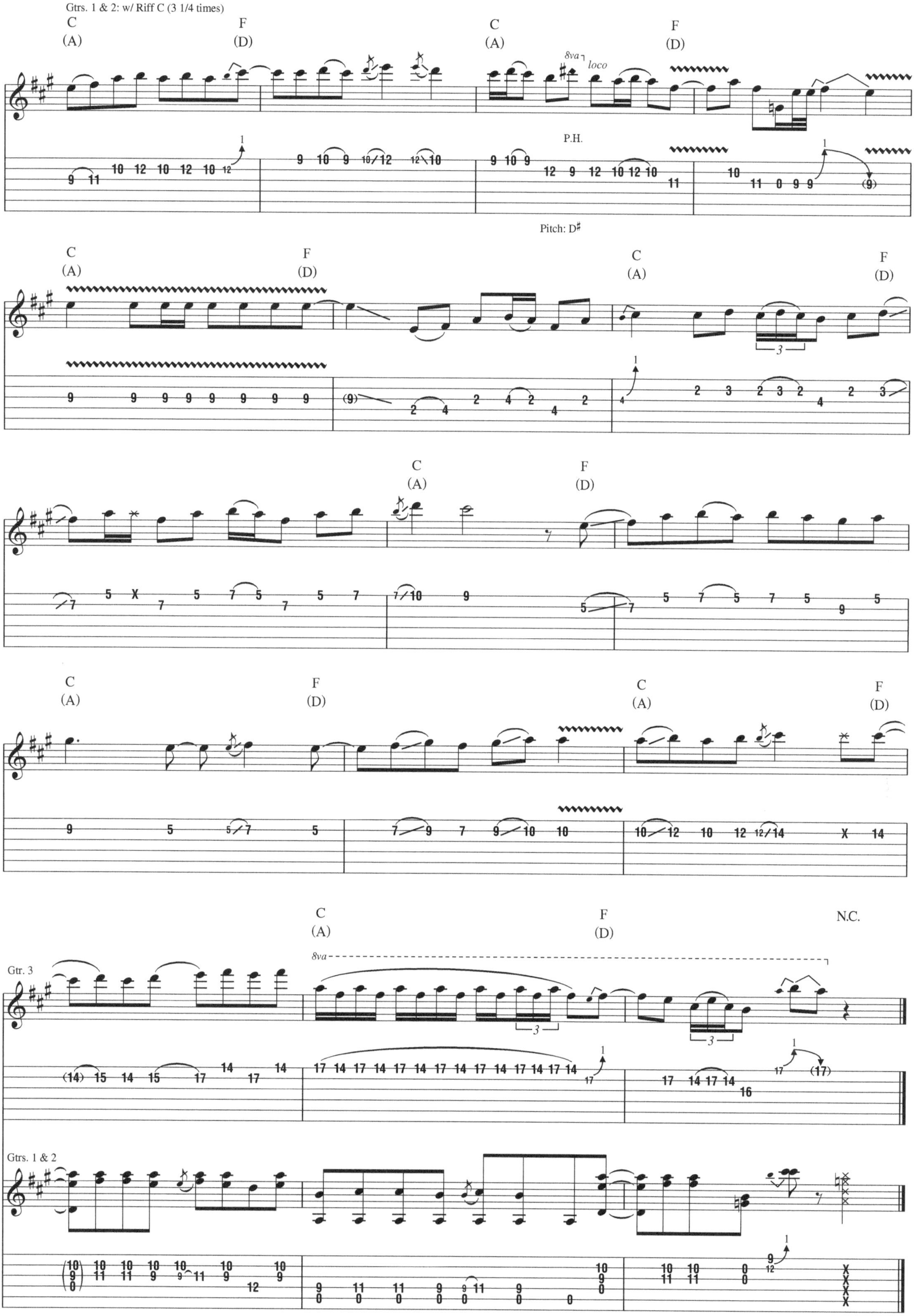

from *Dinosaur*

Forget the Swan
Words and Music by J Mascis

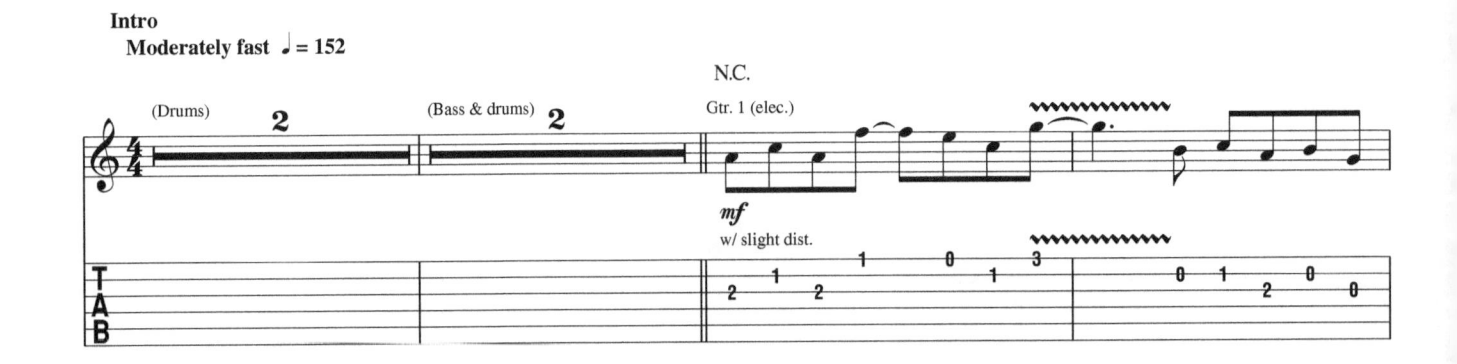

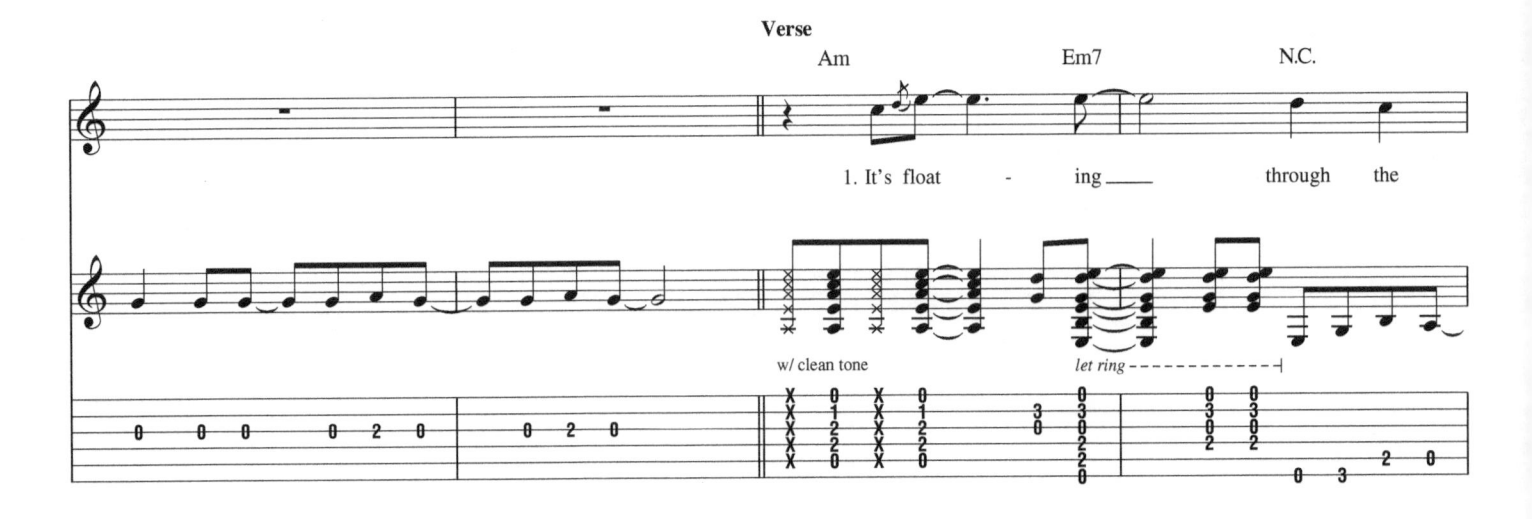

down. Be-ware her wrath, the im-age gone. The shell is crum-bling, fix my frown. This spell would be cl-ear in non-tra-di-tion, and step-ping on these piec-es of pain

Dm7 D7sus4/C B C N.C. C
and smirk. And rape goes through
let ring
Dm7 D7sus4/C B C
to sin my eye - eyes, and shapes know where the heart -
N.C. C Dm7 D7sus4/C Asus2
- ache will lurk.
Gtr. 1
let ring
Gtr. 2 (acous.)
mf

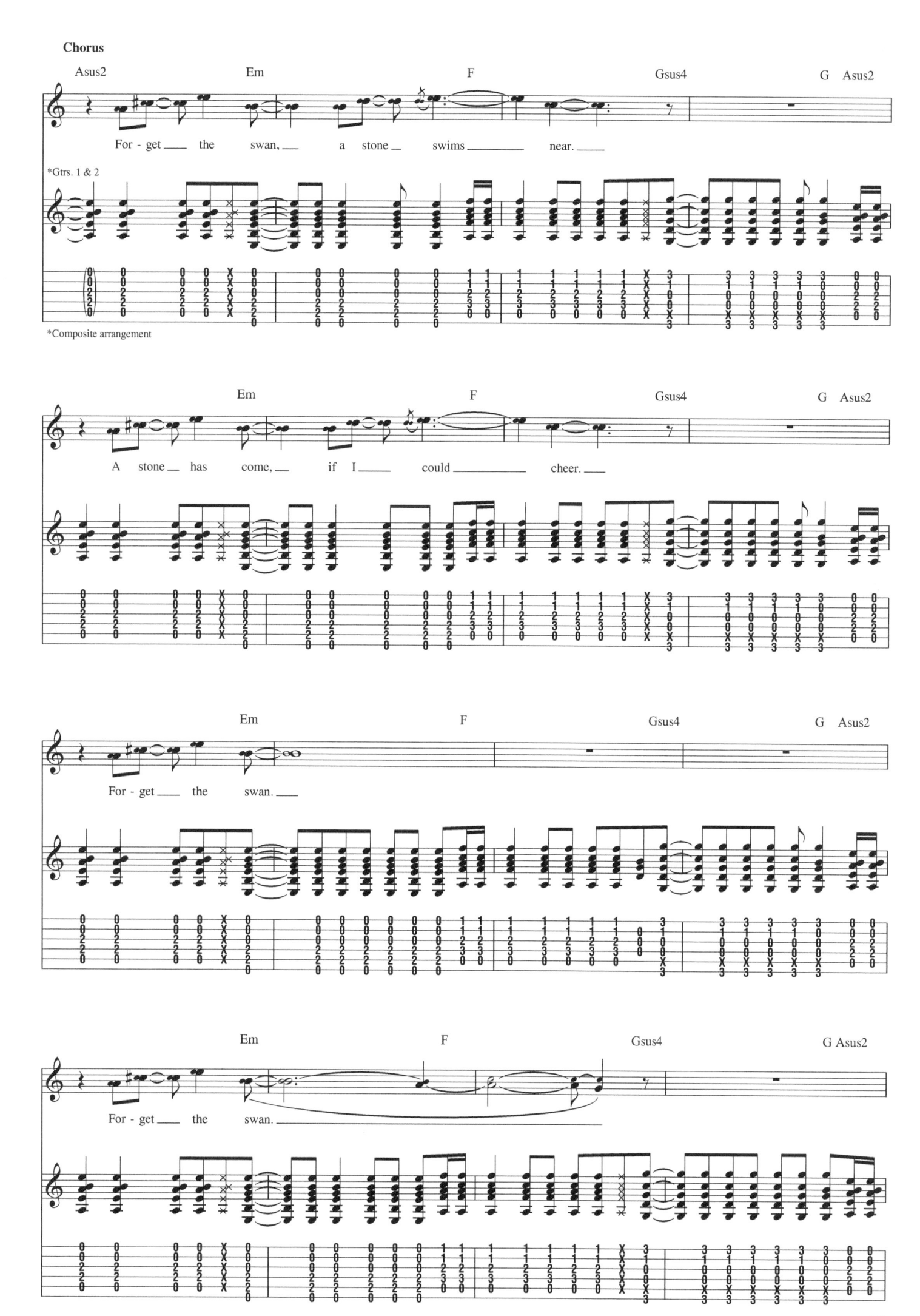

Chorus

Forget the swan, a stone swims near.

*Gtrs. 1 & 2

*Composite arrangement

A stone has come, if I could cheer.

Forget the swan.

Forget the swan.

24

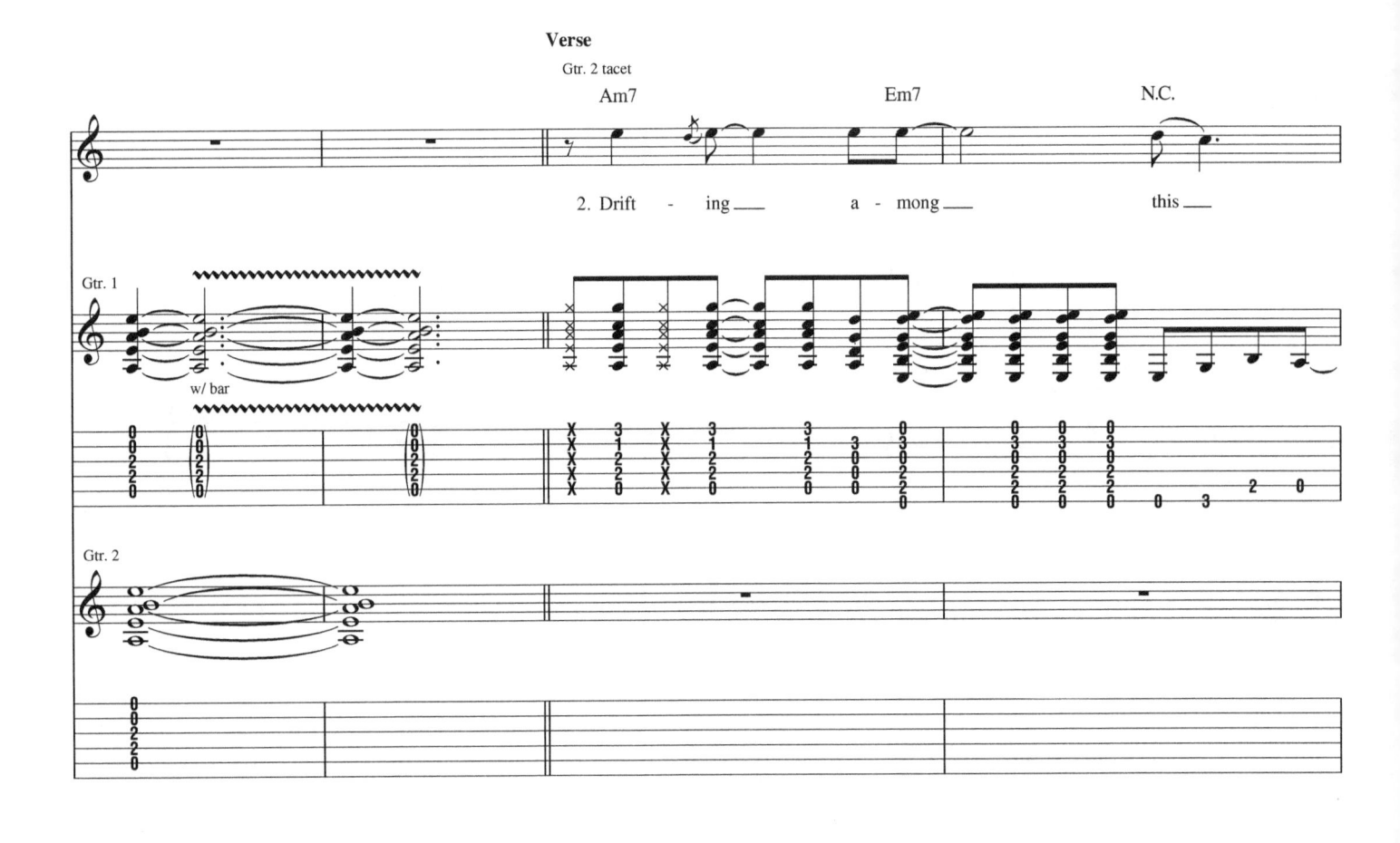

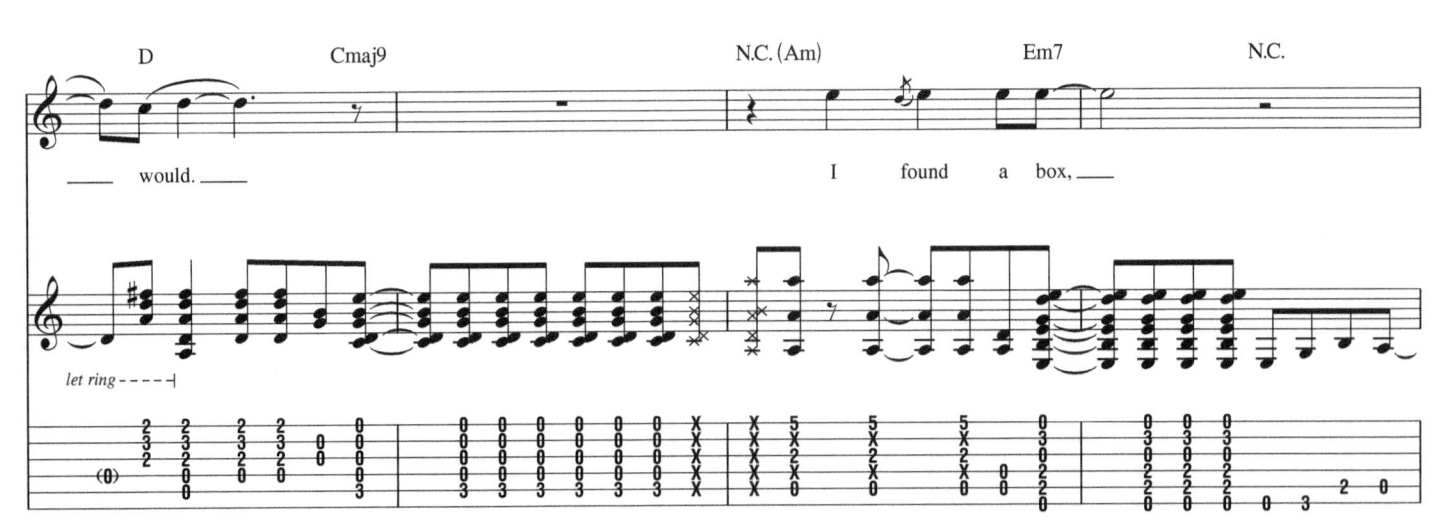

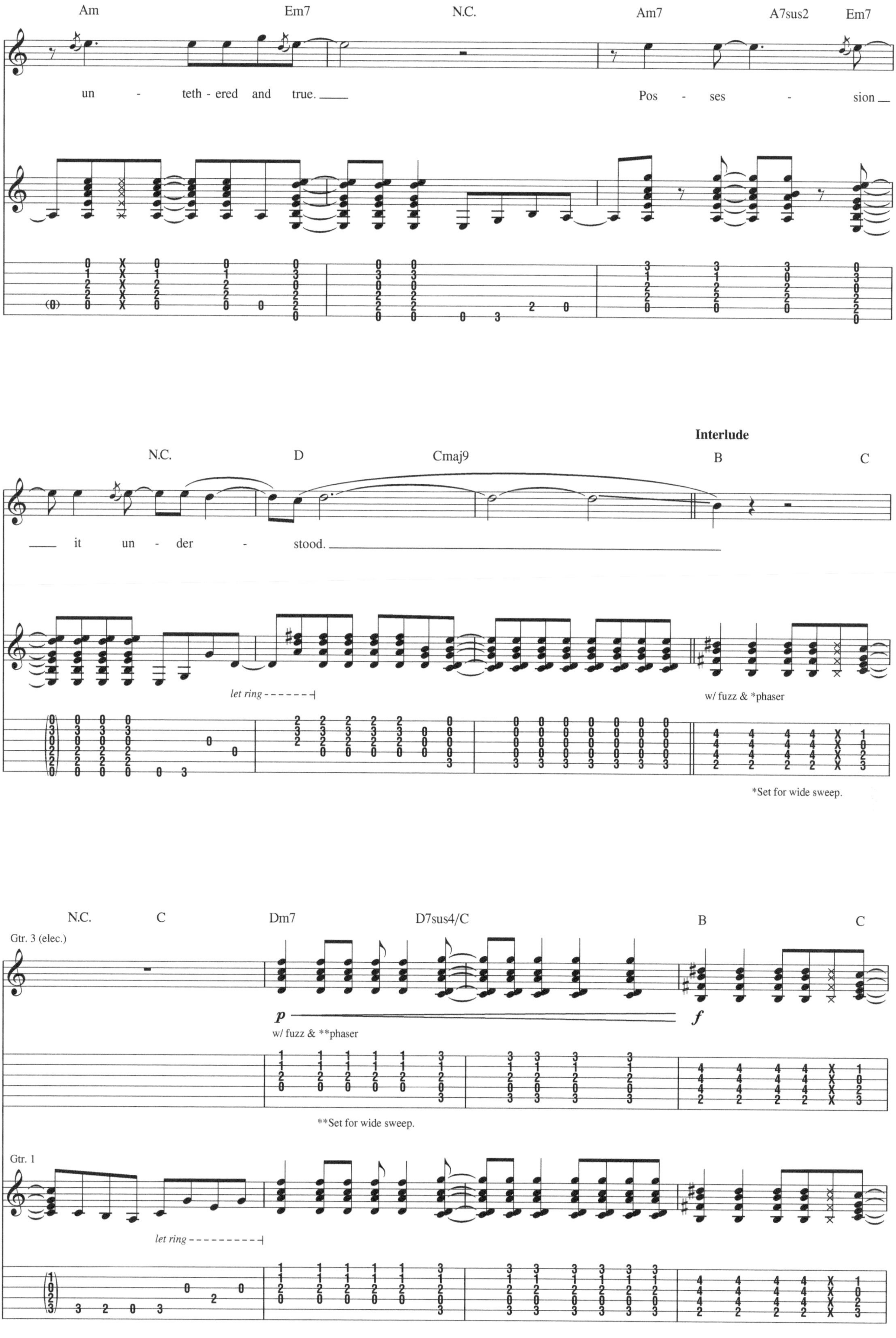
Am
Em7
N.C.
Am7
A7sus2
Em7
un - teth - ered and true.
Pos - ses - sion
N.C.
D
Cmaj9
Interlude
B
C
it un - der - stood.
let ring
w/ fuzz & *phaser
*Set for wide sweep.
N.C.
C
Dm7
D7sus4/C
B
C
Gtr. 3 (elec.)
p
f
w/ fuzz & **phaser
**Set for wide sweep.
Gtr. 1
let ring

Guitar Solo
N.C.
C
Dm7
D7sus4/C
B
C
let ring
N.C.
C
Dm7
D7sus4/C
let ring
B
C
N.C.
C
Dm7
D7sus4/C
let ring
fuzz & phaser off

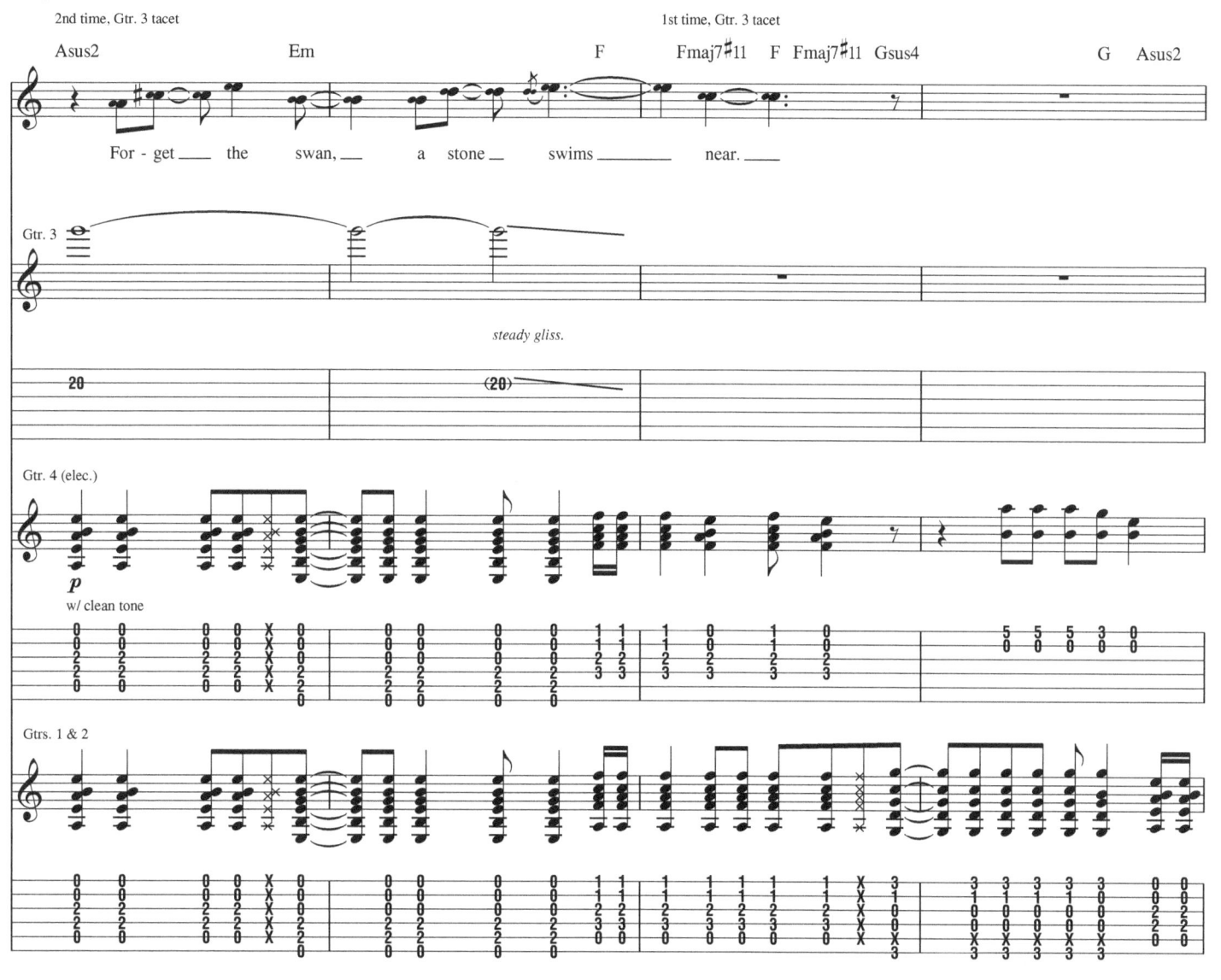

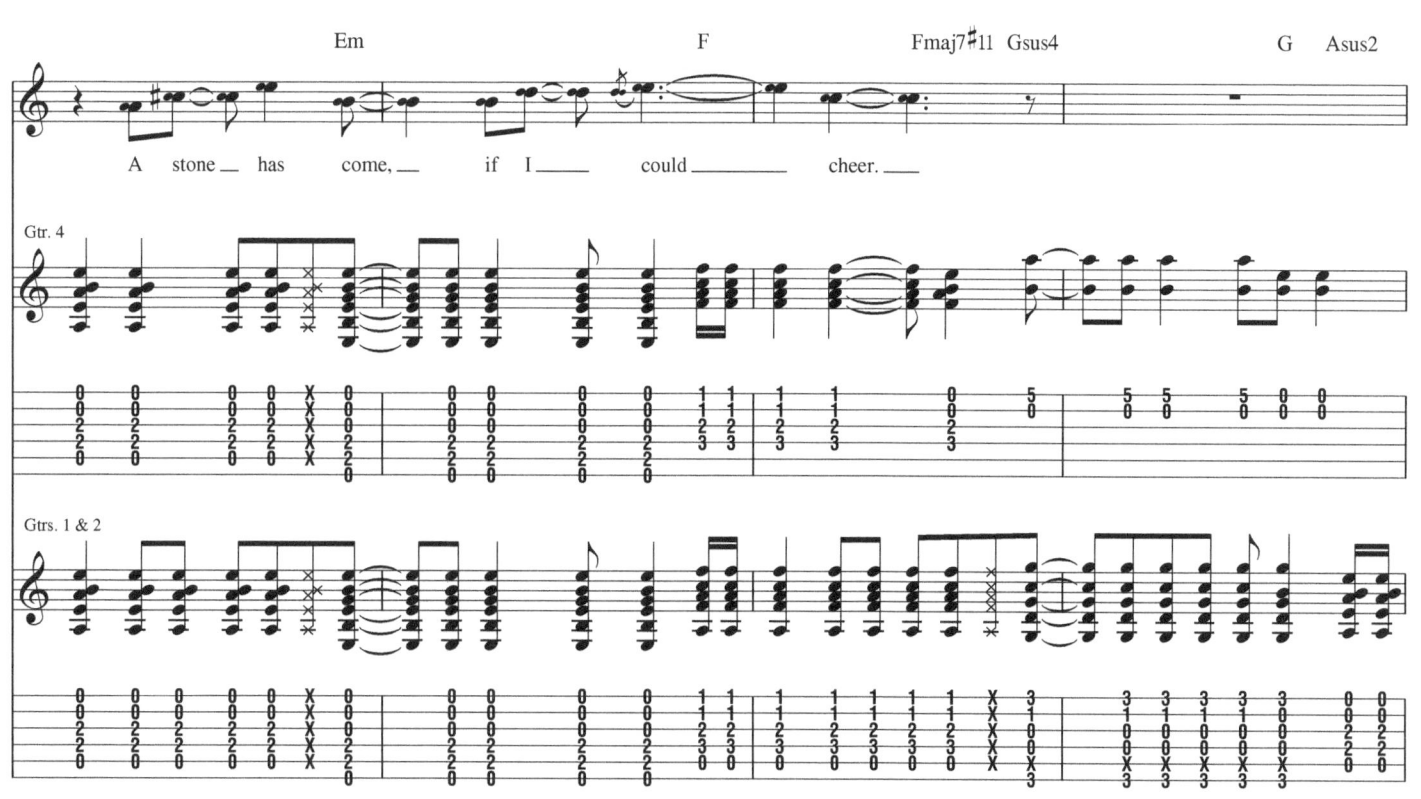

Chorus

2nd time, Gtr. 3 tacet

Forget the swan, a stone swims near.

A stone has come, if I could cheer.

To Coda
Em
F
Fmaj7♯11
Gsus4
G
Asus2
For - get the swan.
Em
F
Fmaj9♯11
Fmaj7♯11
Gsus4
G
Asus2
For - get the swan.
Interlude
Gtr. 4 tacet
Gtr. 2 tacet
N.C.
Gtr. 1
w/ bar
w/ slight dist.
Gtr. 2

Bridge

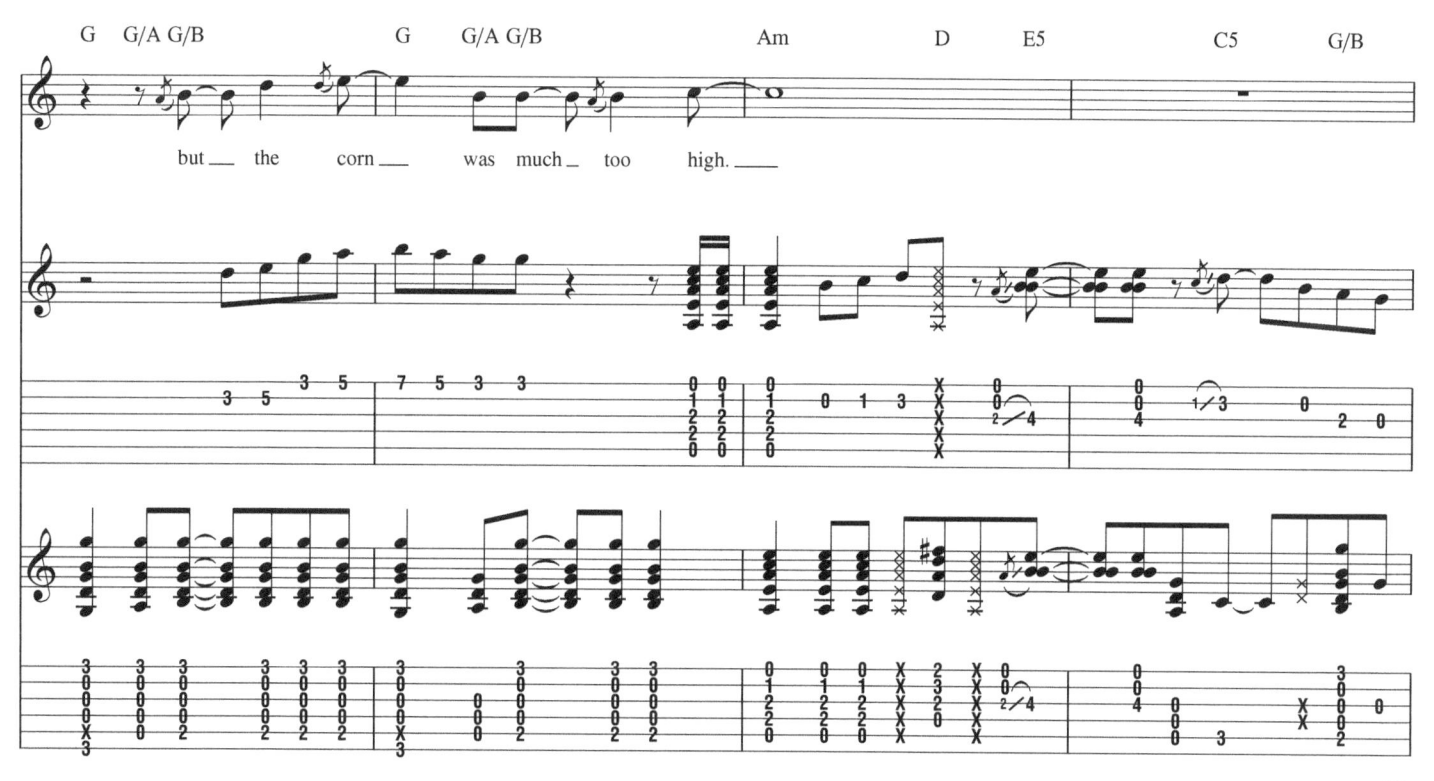

How I tried to warn my neighbor,

but the corn was much too high.

G G/A G/B G G/A G/B Am D E5 Cmaj7 G/B
In con - fu - sion, up and threw him; woke up ev - 'ry day. But
let ring
D.S. al Coda
G G/A G/B G G/A G/B Am D E5 Cmaj7 G/B Asus2
it's not too late, broth - er, I'll still say you were mine.
Gtr. 4
Gtr. 1
let ring
Gtr. 2

Coda
Em
F
For - get the swan.
Fmaj9♯11 Fmaj7♯11
Gsus4
G N.C.
Breakdown
Gtr. 4 tacet
Asus2 N.C.
For - get the swan,
the dreams are gone. The pain goes on.
Asus2
(They fly at
Gtrs. 1 & 2

Outro-Guitar Solo

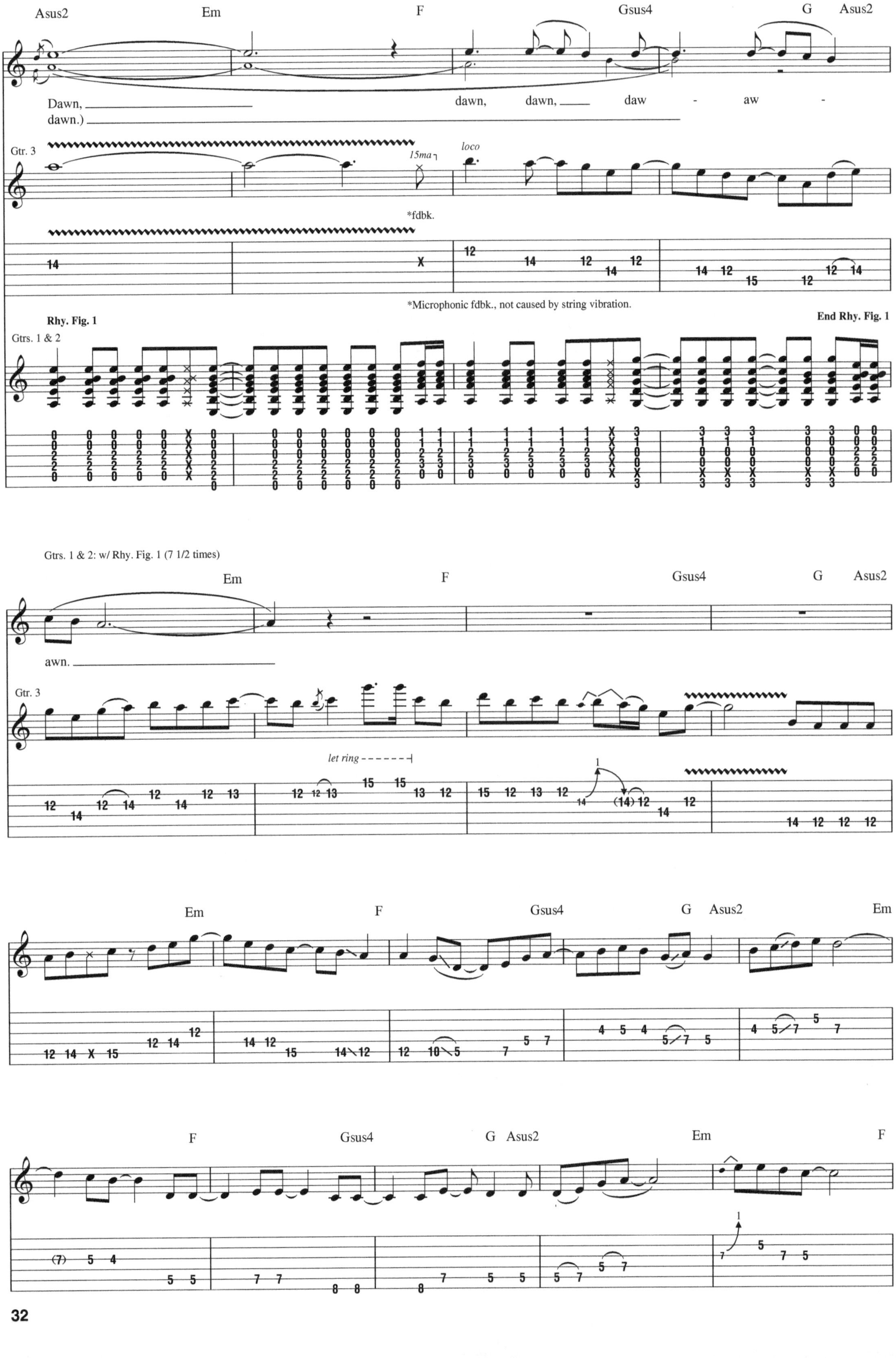

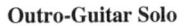

Gsus4
G
Asus2
Em
F
Gtr. 3 tacet
Gsus4
G
Asus2
Em
F
For - get the swan.
*Gtr. 5 (elec.)
Gtr. 3
divisi
Gtr. 5
*w/ fuzz, played f.
Gsus4
G
Asus2
Em
F
For - get the swan.
Gsus4
G
Asus2
Em
F
For - get the swan.

Fsus2 Gsus4
G Asus2
Em
F
For - get the swan,
Gtr. 5
Gtrs. 1 & 2

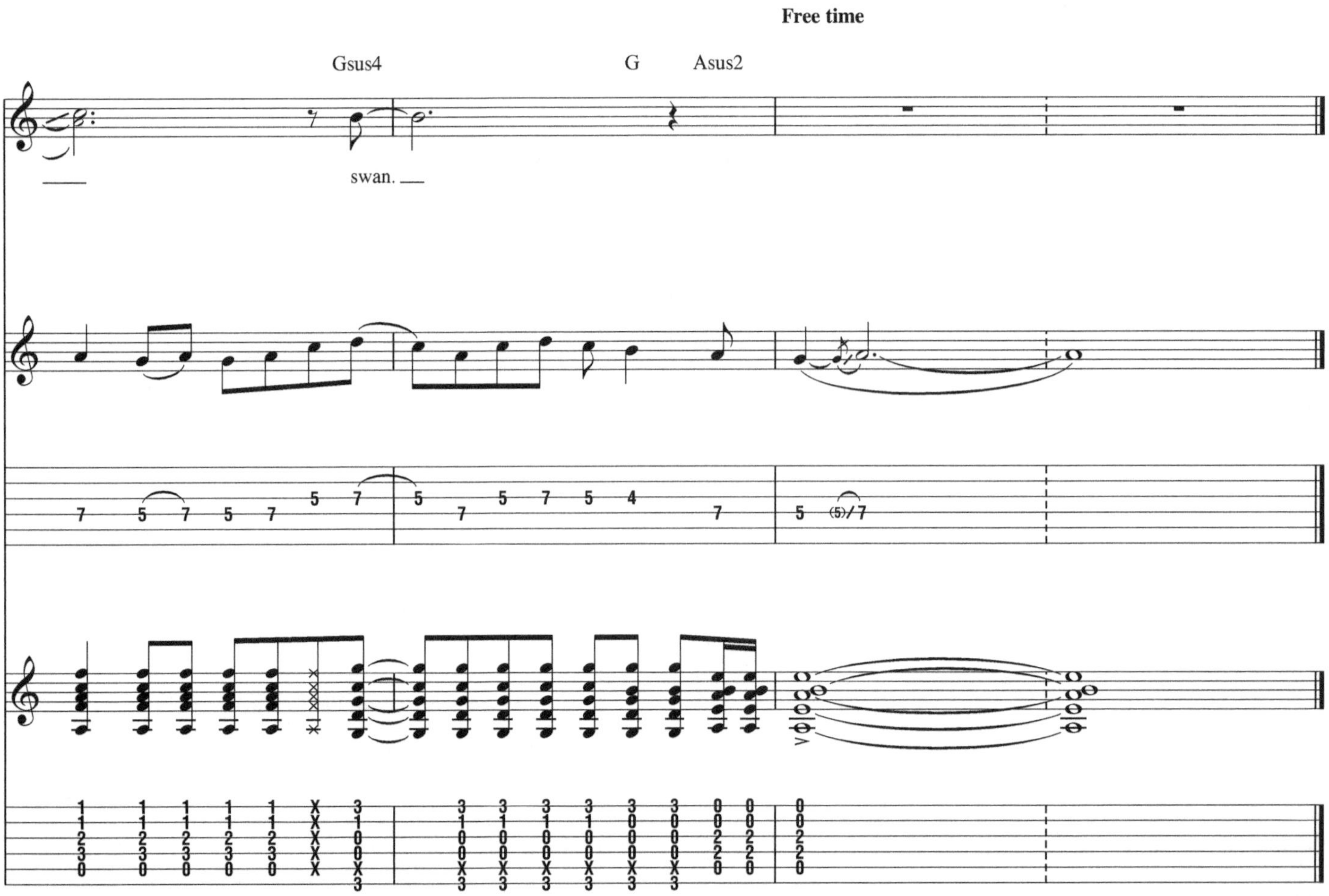
Free time
Gsus4
G Asus2
swan.

from *Bug*

Freak Scene

Words and Music by J Mascis

Intro

Moderately fast ♩ = 156

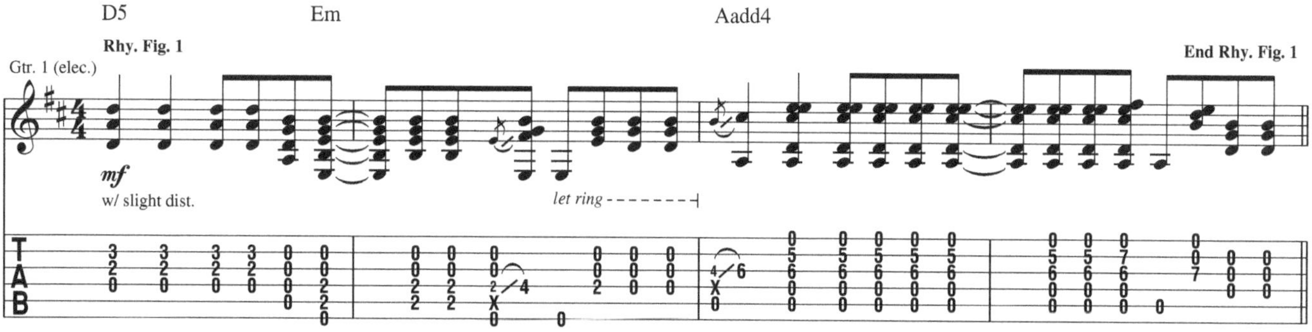

Verse

Gtr. 1: w/ Rhy. Fig. 1 (4 times)

Gtr. 2: w/ Rhy. Fig. 2 (3 times)

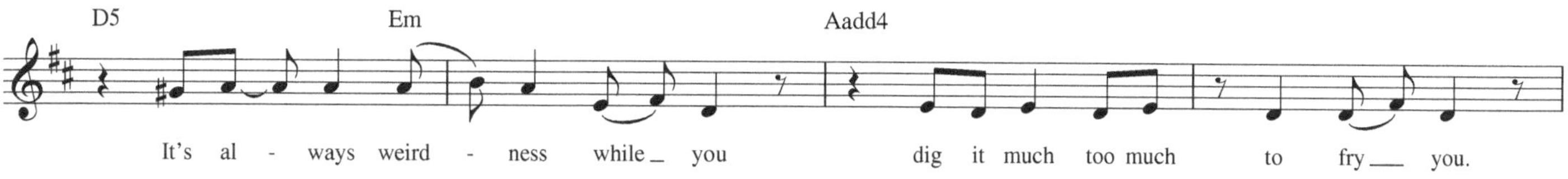

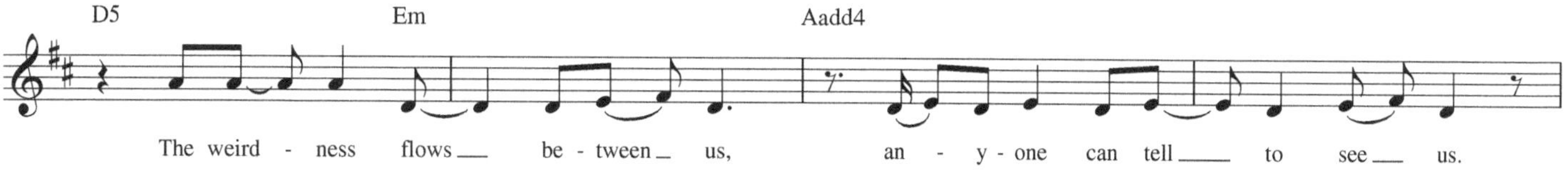

D5 Em Aadd4
Freak scene just can't be - lieve us, why can't it just be cool and free us?
Gtr. 3 (elec.)
f
w/ dist.
D/A
Gtr. 1
Gtr. 3
8va
loco
fdbk.
Interlude
E5 Esus2 E5 Esus2 E5 E Esus2 E5 Aadd9
Play 4 times
Gtr. 1
Gtr. 3
P.M.
Gtr. 2

2. Seen enough to eye you, but I've seen too much to try you.

It's always weirdness while you dig it much too much to fry you.

The weirdness flows between us, anyone can tell to see us.

Freak scene just can't believe us, can't it just be cool and leave us?

3. So fucked I can't believe it.

Lyrics:

Aadd4 — If there's a way I wish we'd see it.
D5 Em — How it could work, just can't conceive it.

Aadd4 — A, what a mess just to leave it.

Guitar Solo
Gtr. 2: w/ Rhy. Fig. 2 (6 times)

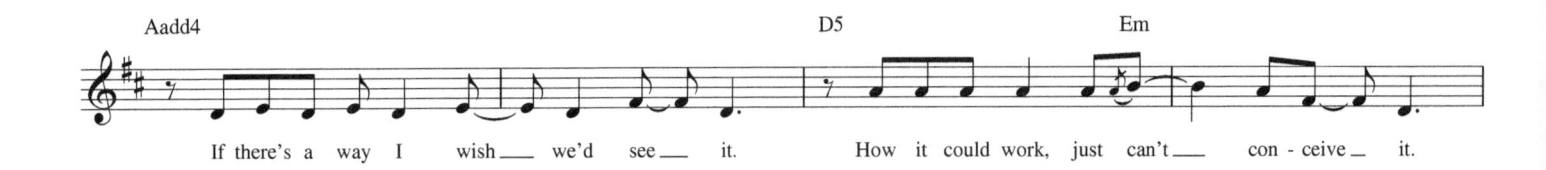

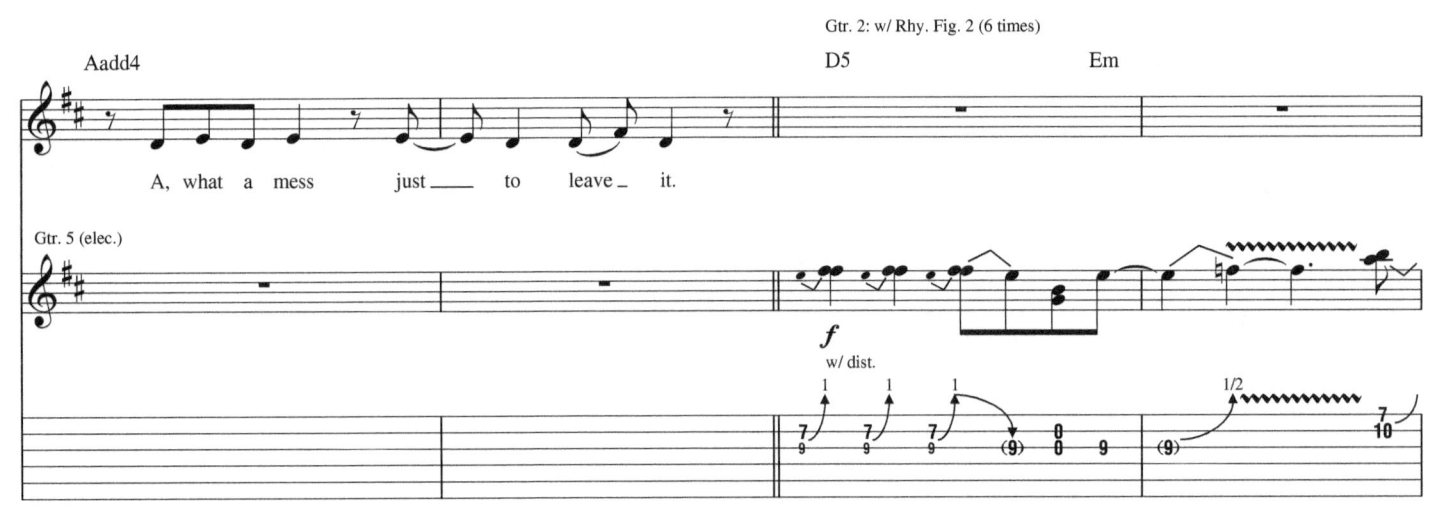

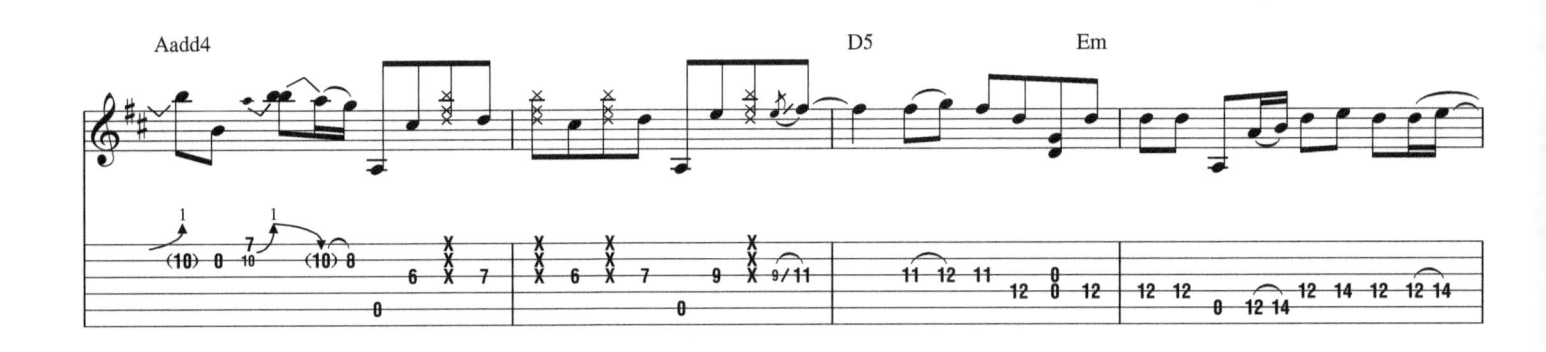

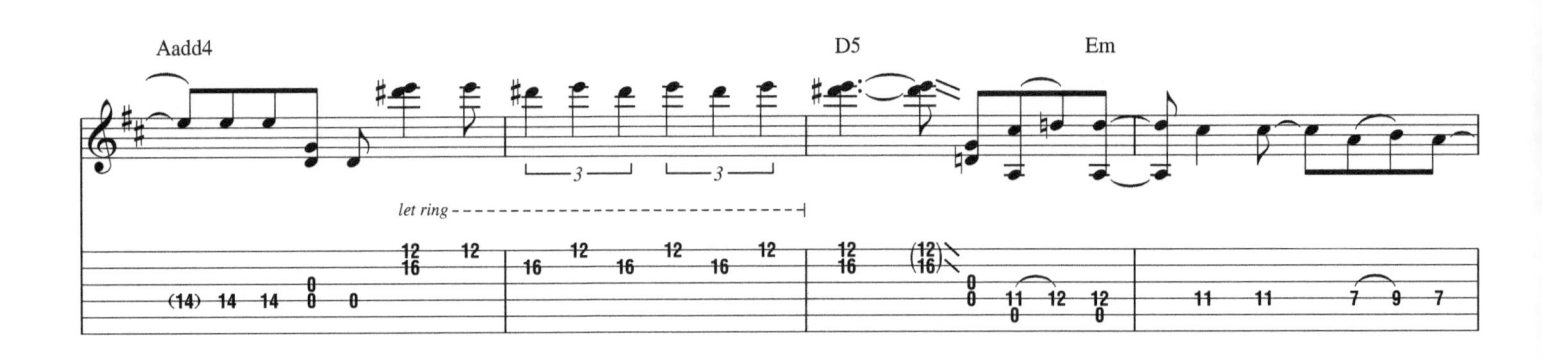

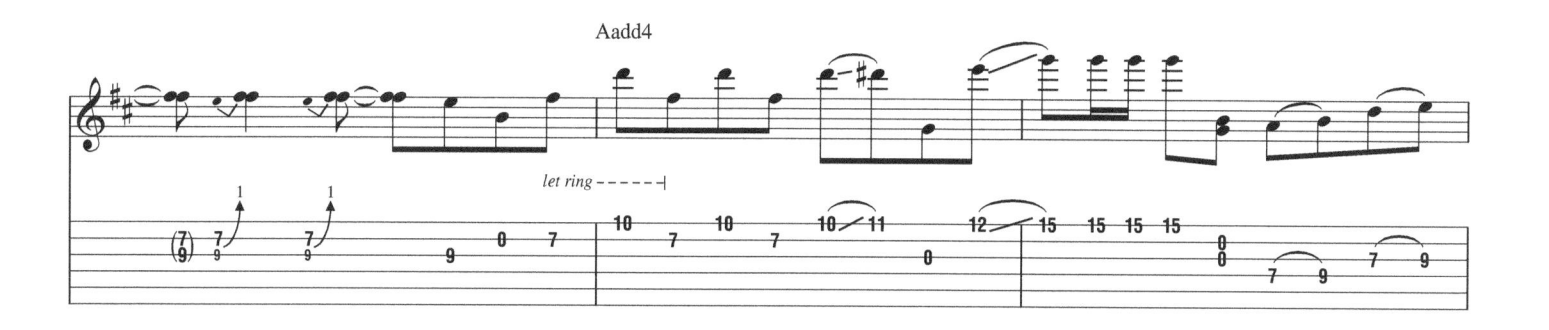

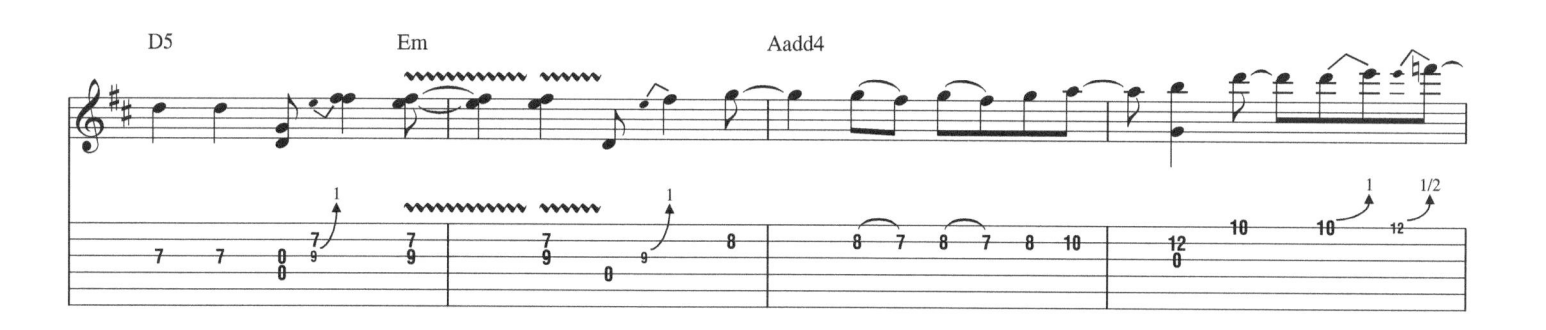

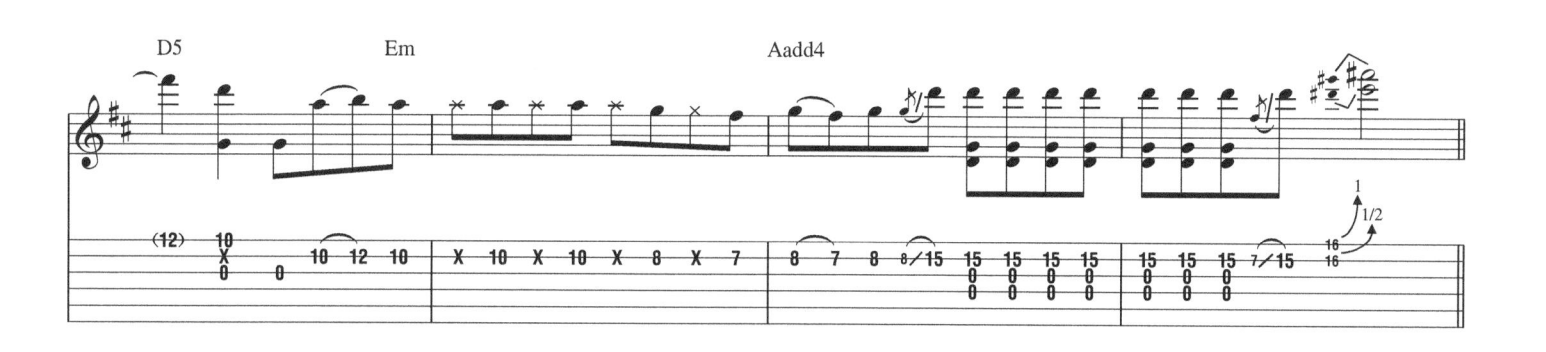

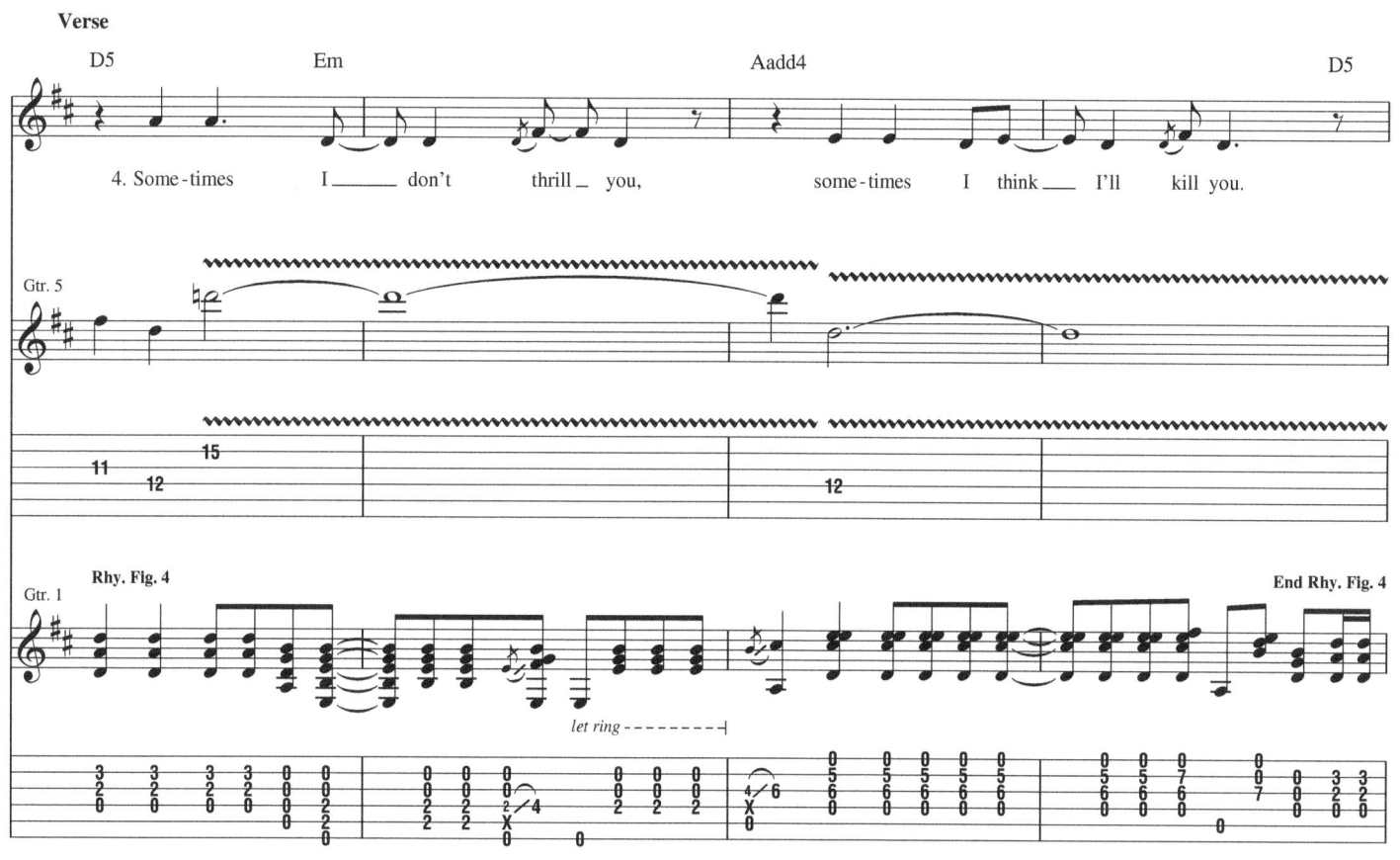

4. Sometimes I ___ don't thrill ___ you, sometimes I think ___ I'll kill you.

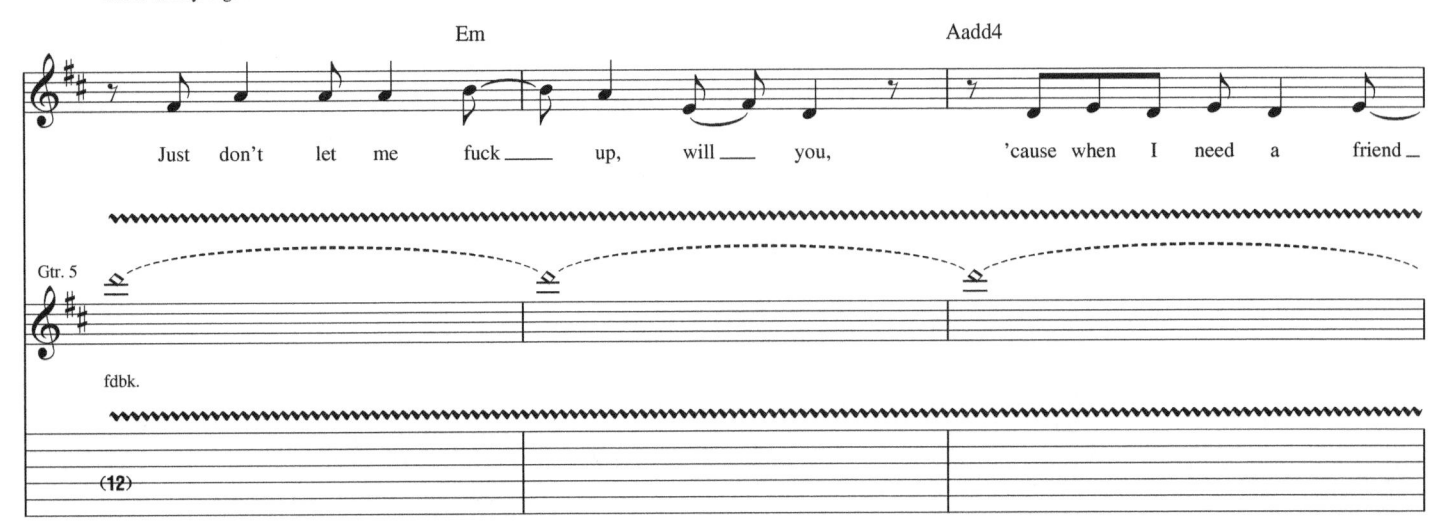

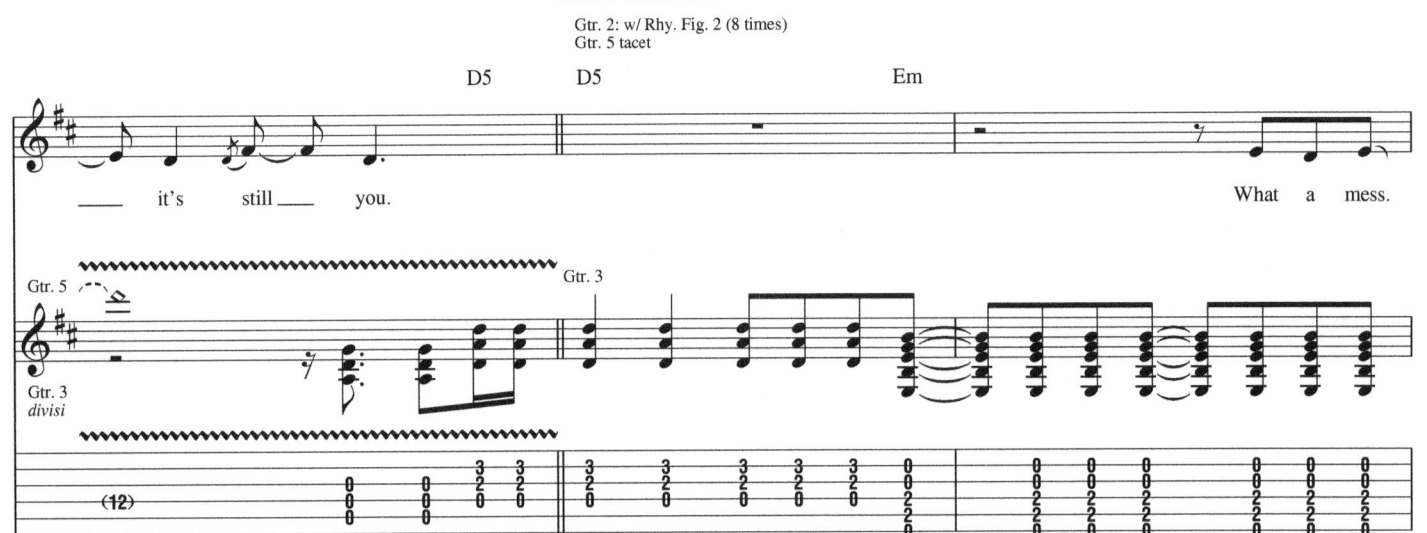

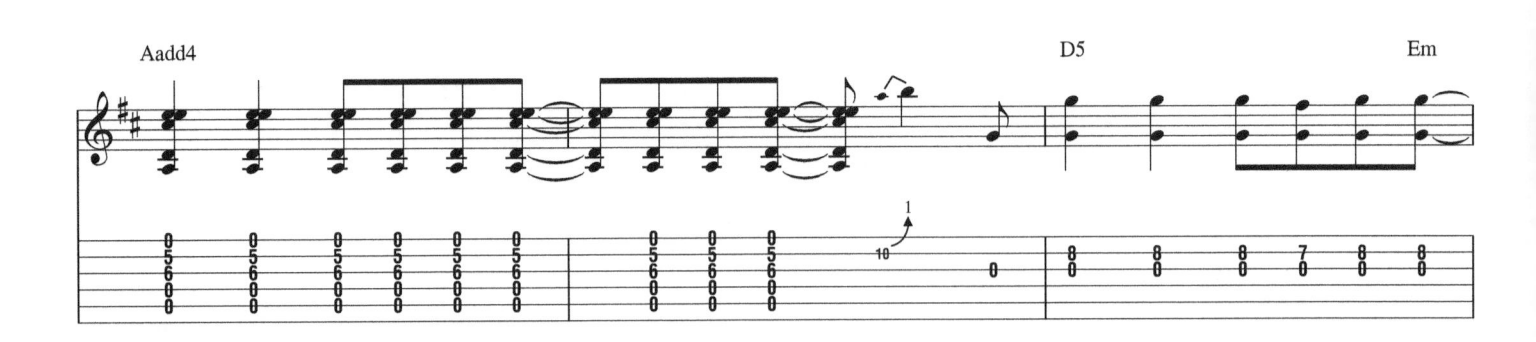

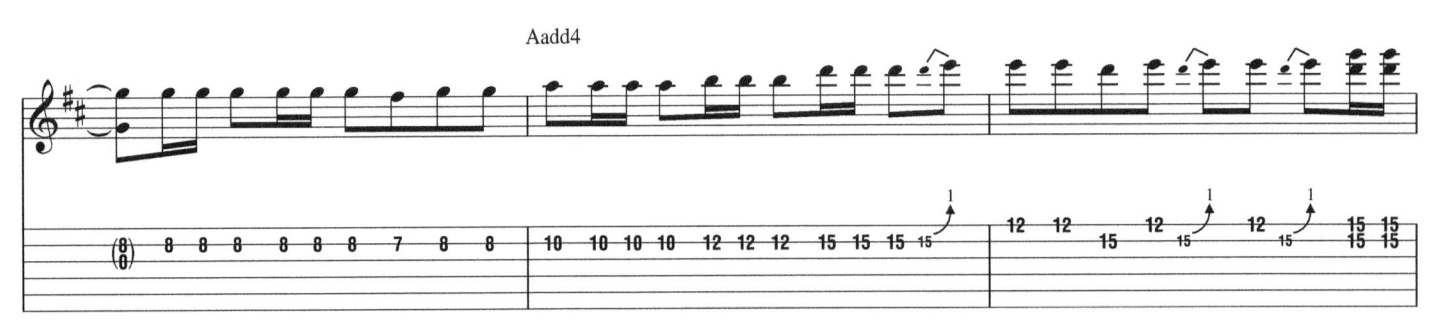

Just don't let me fuck up, will you, 'cause when I need a friend it's still you. What a mess.

Outro-Guitar Solo

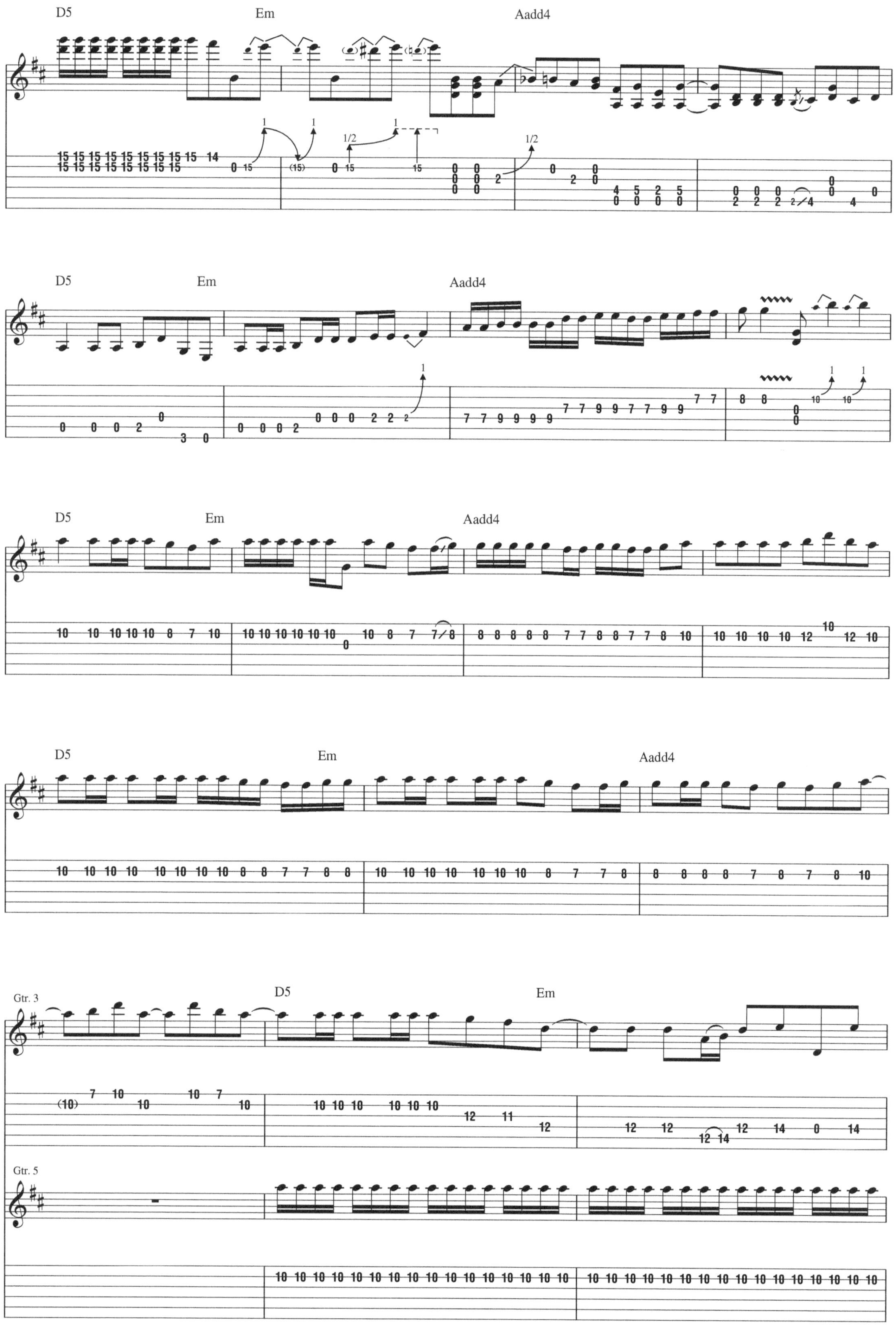
D5
Em
Aadd4
D5
Em
Aadd4
D5
Em
Aadd4
D5
Em
Aadd4
Gtr. 3
D5
Em
Gtr. 5

Aadd4
D5
Em
Aadd4
D5
Free time
Begin fade
Fade out
8va
loco
Gtr. 3
fdbk.
Pitch: G
E
Gtrs. 2 & 5
fdbk.
Pitch: F♯

from *You're Living All Over Me*

Little Fury Things

Words and Music by J Mascis

Capo II

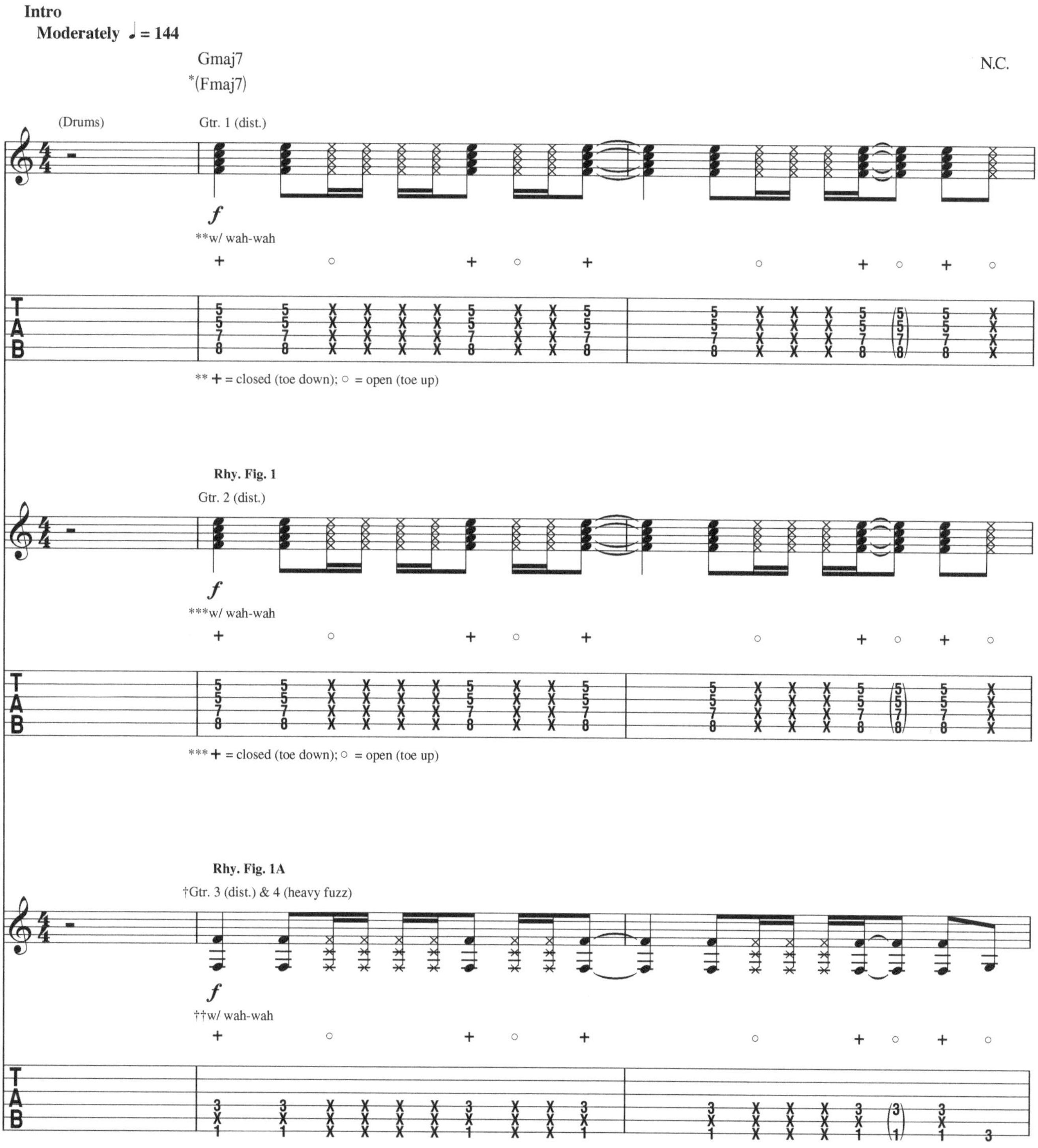

*Symbols in parentheses represent chord names respective to capoed guitar. Symbols above reflect actual sounding chords. Capoed fret is "0" in tab.

†Composite arrangement; Gtr. 4 omits wah-wah.

†† + = closed (toe down); ○ = open (toe up)

Bm (Am)
B5 (A5)
Bm (Am)
B5 (A5)
Shouted: What is it?!
let ring
End Rhy. Fig. 1
End Rhy. Fig. 1A
Gtr. 2: w/ Rhy. Fig. 1 (1 1/2 times)
Gtrs. 3 & 4: w/ Rhy. Fig. 1A (2 1/2 times)
Gmaj7 (Fmaj7)
N.C.
Bm (Am)
B5 (A5)
Bm (Am)
Gtr. 1
let ring
B5 (A5)
Gmaj7 (Fmaj7)
Who is it?!
let ring

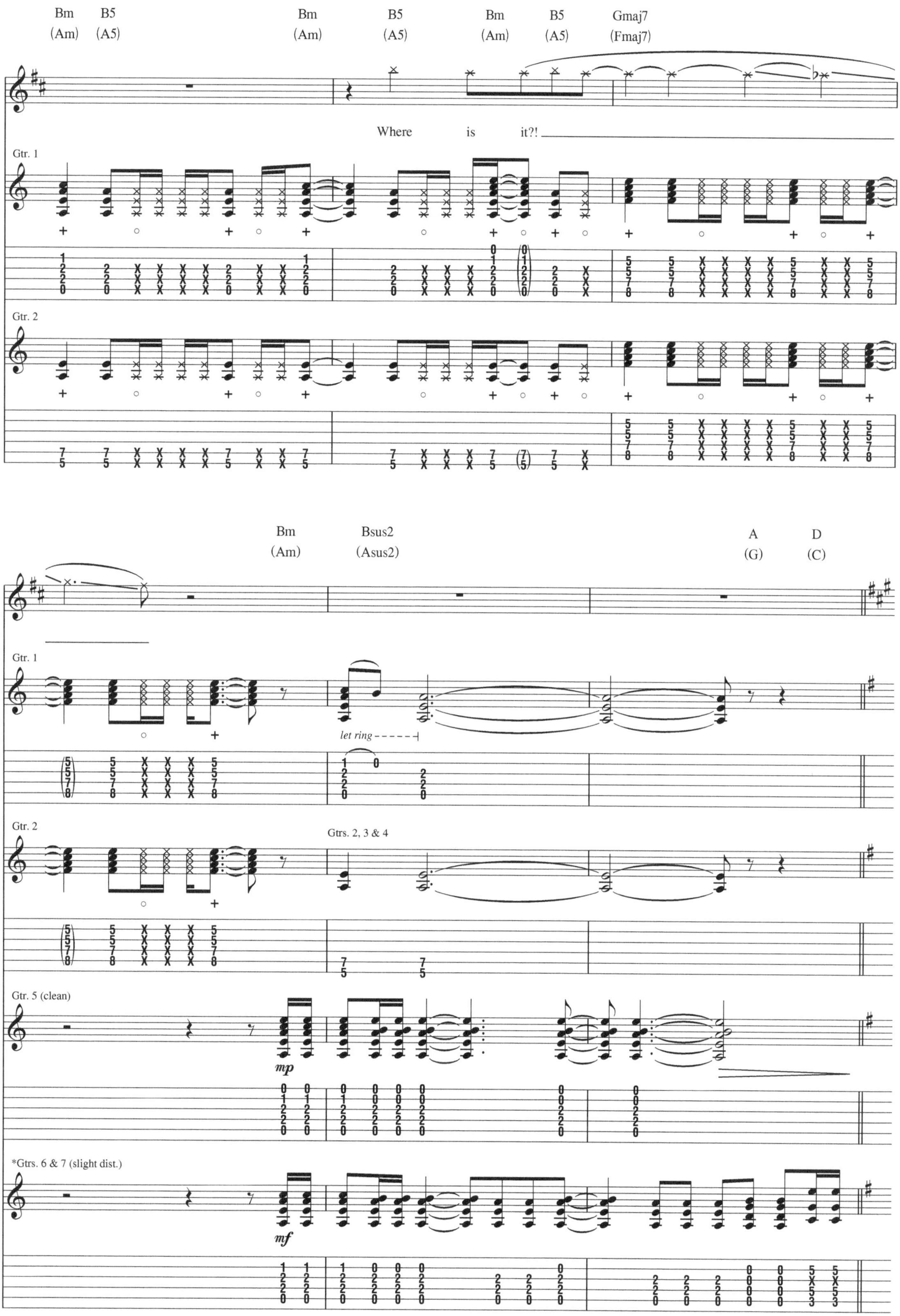

*Composite arrangement

46

47

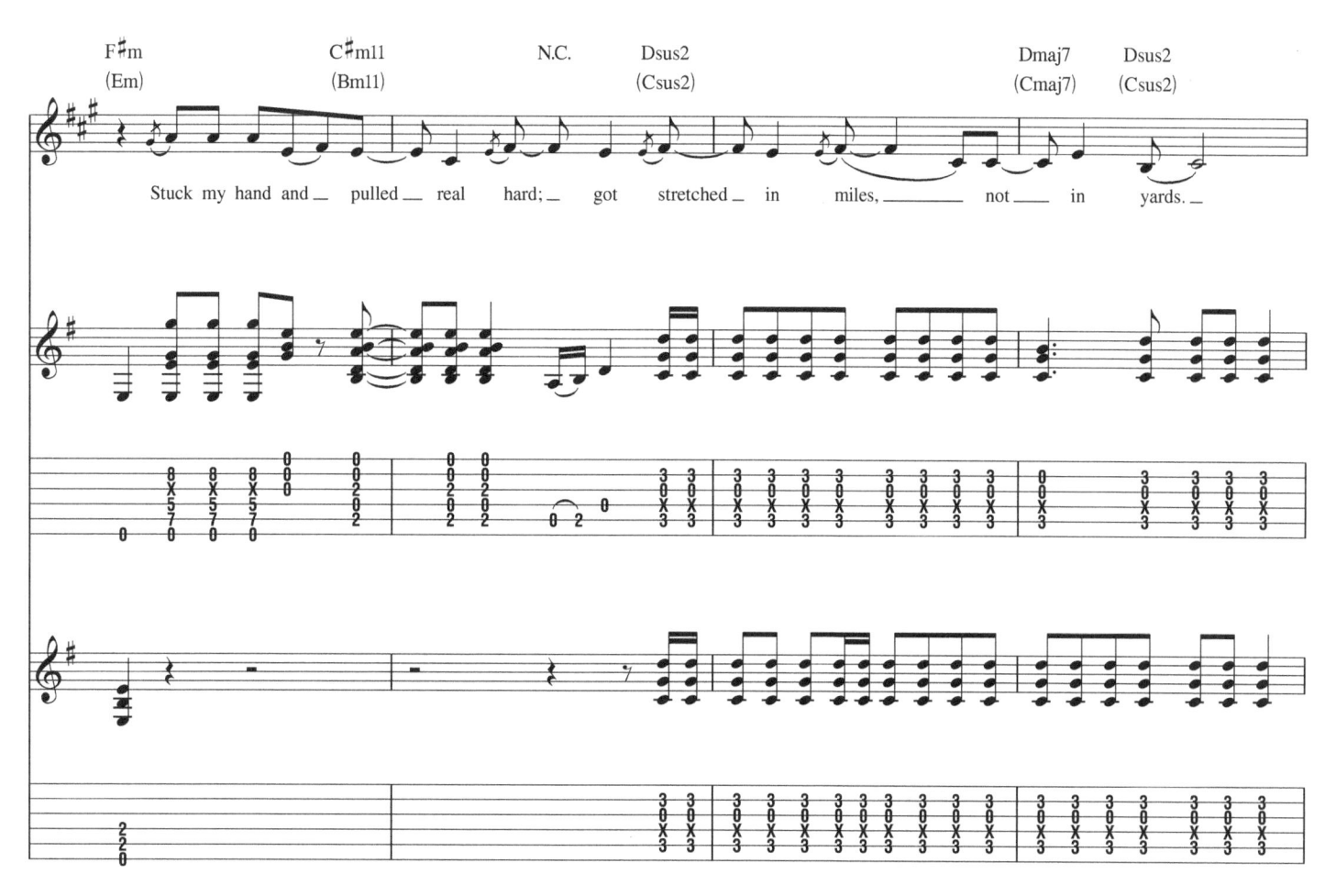

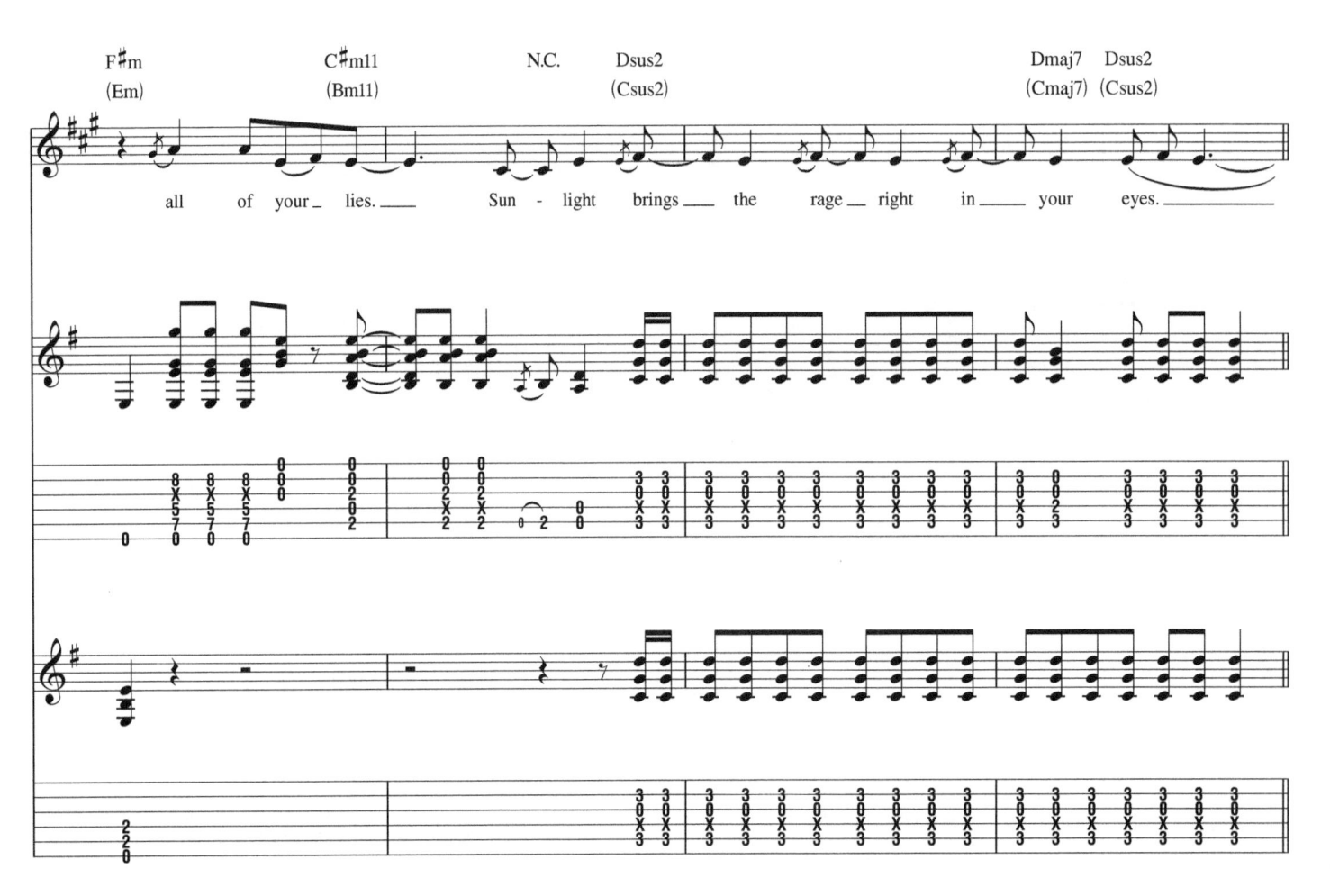

Then I read ___ a - bout all those ___ who be - lieve ___ all of your ___ lies. ___ Sun - light brings ___ the rage ___ right in ___ your eyes. ___

Interlude

Gtr. 7 tacet
A (G)
Dmaj7 (Cmaj7)
D (C)
Dadd9 (Cadd9)
Dmaj9 (Cmaj9)
*Gtrs. 6 & 8
let ring
*Composite arrangement
Gtr. 6 tacet
F♯m11 (Em11)
C♯m11 (Bm11)
N.C.
**Gtrs. 8 & 9
P.M.
**Gtr. 9 (dist.), played f.
D.S. al Coda
w/ bar
-1 1/2
-2 1/2

Coda
Chorus
Gtrs. 6 & 7: w/ Rhy. Fig. 2
C♯m11 (Bm11) Dadd2 (Cadd2) D (C) D (C) F♯m (Em) E (D) Esus4 (Dsus4) E (D)
fast - er than I crawl. A rab - bit falls a - way from me,
Gtrs. 6 & 7
*Gtrs. 10 & 11 (heavy fuzz)
15ma
loco
Harm.
**
Pitch: G
*Composite arrangement
**Harmonic located approx. one-third the distance between 2nd & 3rd frets. Fret with fleshy part of index finger.
C♯m11 (Bm11) Dadd2 (Cadd2) D (C) F♯m (Em) E (D) Esus4 (Dsus4) E (D)
guess I'll crawl. A rab - bit al - ways smash - es me,
Gtrs. 10 & 11
let ring
C♯m11 (Bm11) Dadd2 (Cadd2) D (C) F♯m (Em) E (D) Esus4 (Dsus4) E (D)
a - gain I crawl. Tried to think what's o - ver me,

it makes me crawl. Then she runs a-way from me

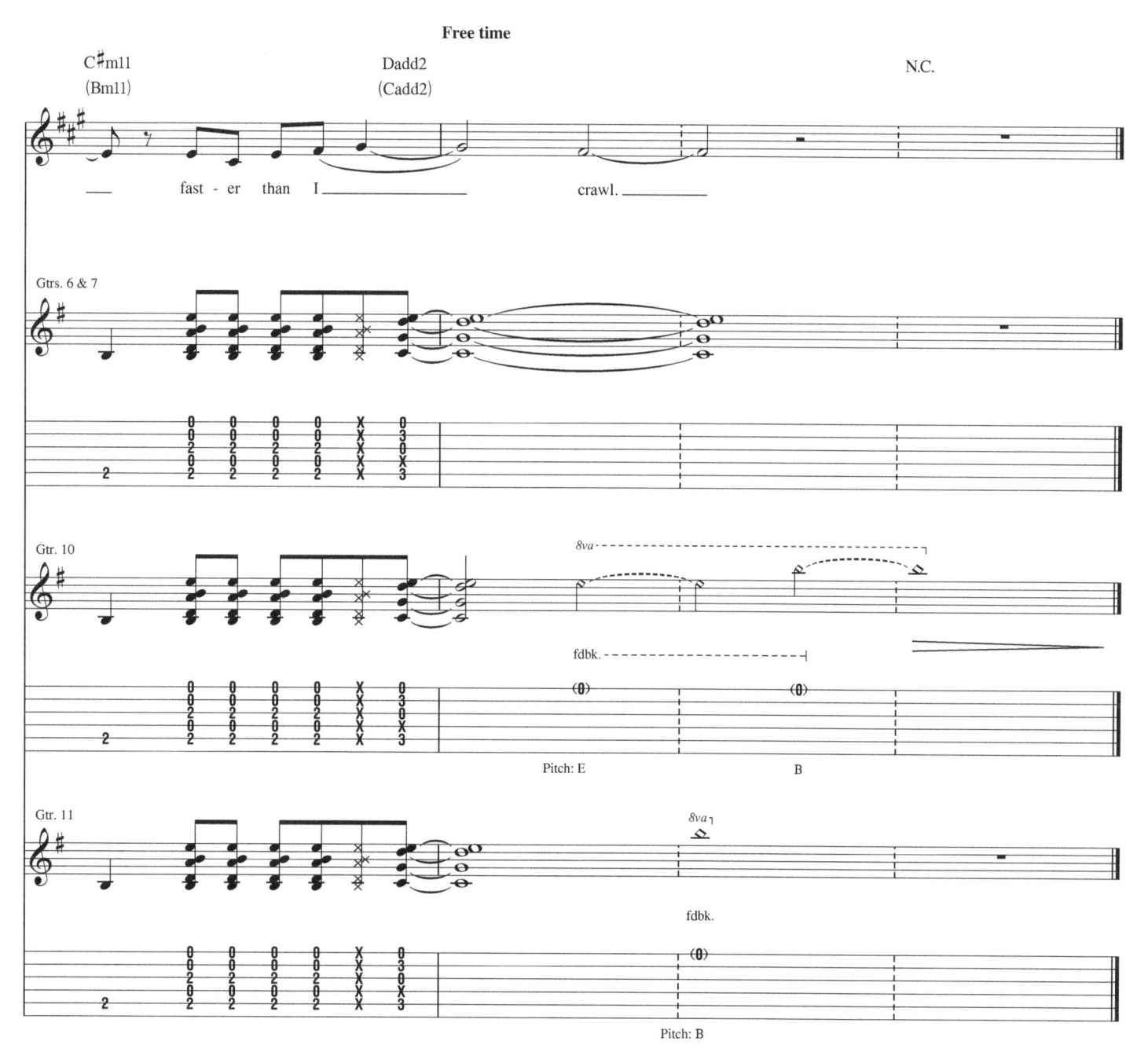

faster than I crawl.

Not You Again

from *Whatever's Cool With Me*

Words and Music by J Mascis

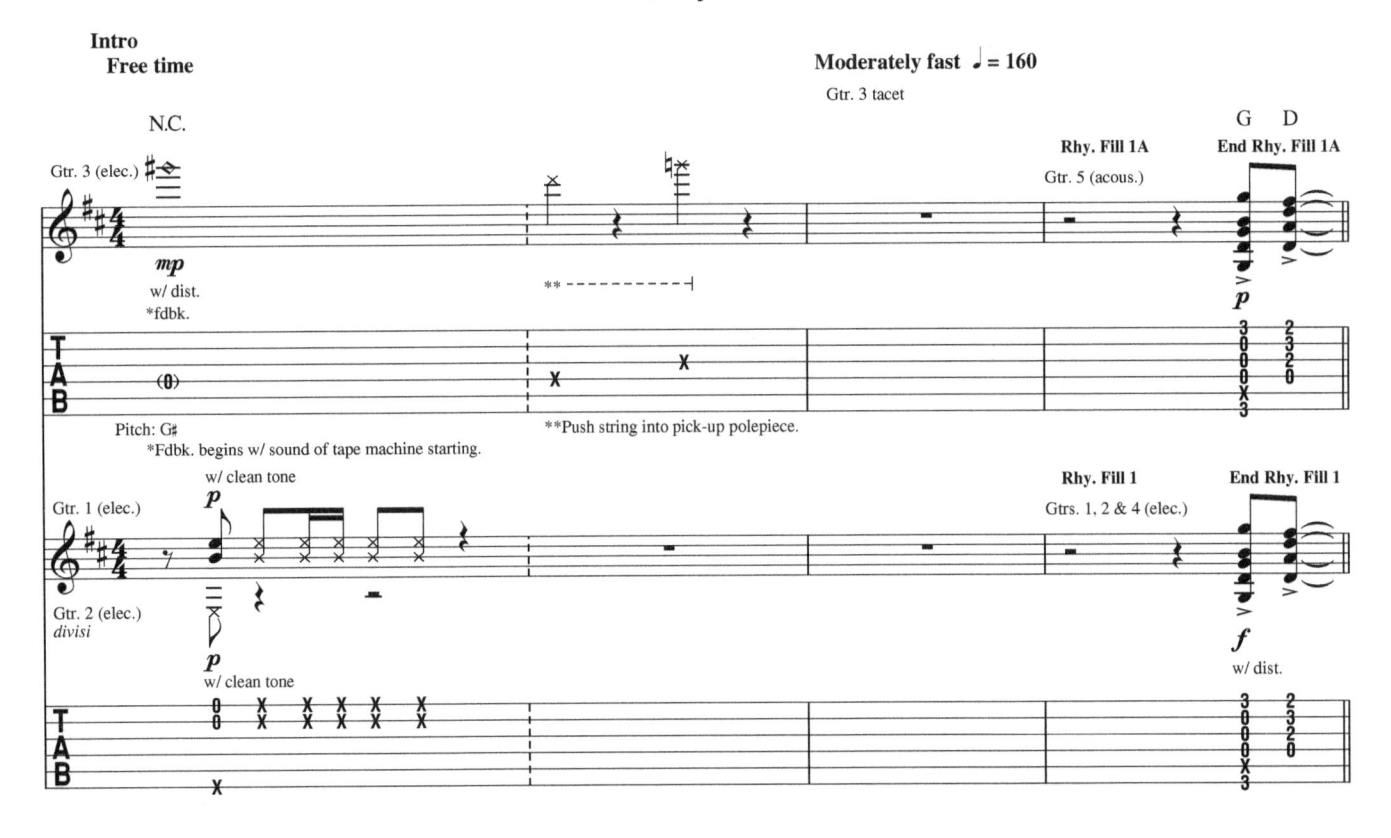

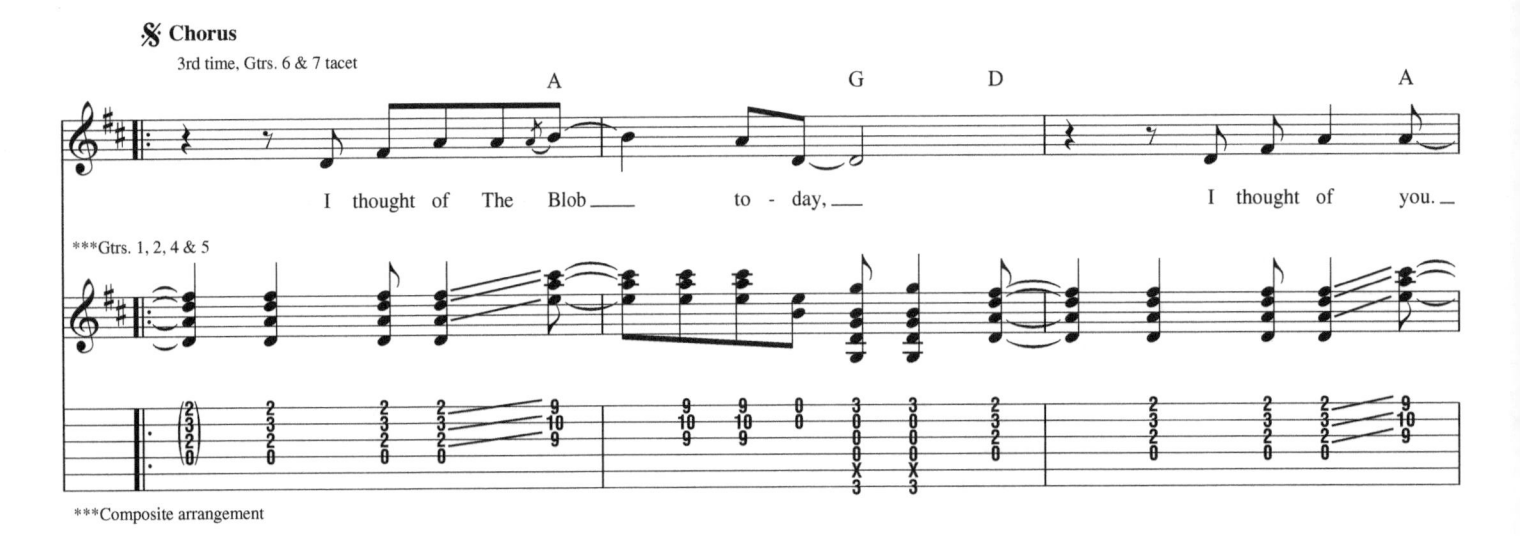

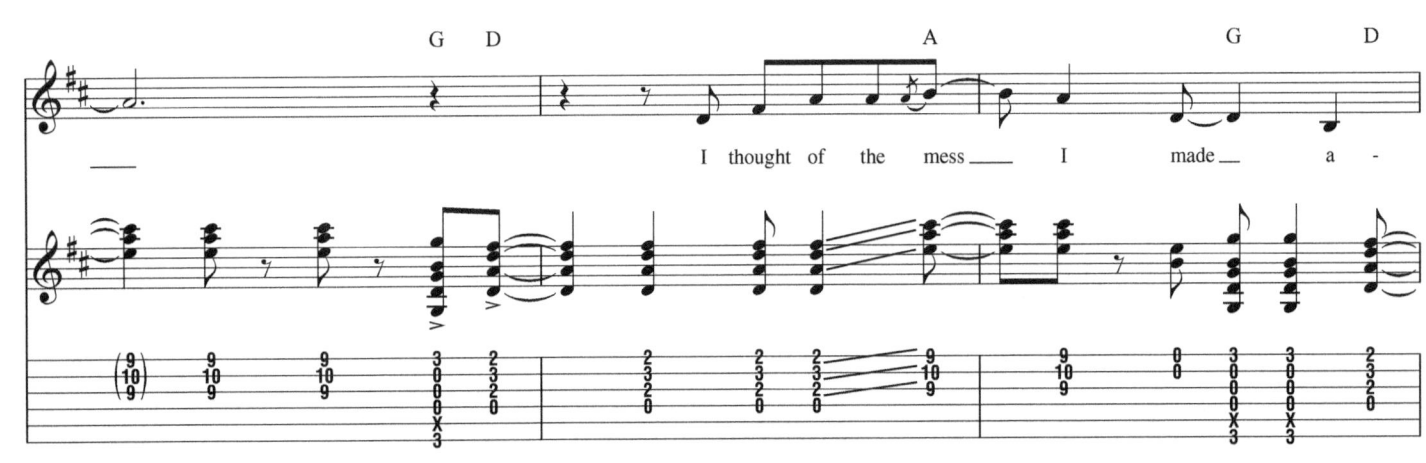

To Coda
Verse
Gtrs. 4 & 5 tacet
A
D
B5
gain. How do I ___ do it?
1. Now when it leaves ___
2. I ___ got no ___
*Gtrs. 1 & 2
*Composite arrangement
E
G
___ your hand, ___ just un - der - stand ___ that I'm ___ the one ___ it missed. ___
___ ad - vice ___ a - bout an - y - thing, ___ just fuck ___ it up ___ your - self. ___
D
B5
E
G
___ Right through a piece ___ I've been ___ keep - in' ___ a - way ___ you ___
___ Is she the kind ___ of girl ___ that's worth ___ get - ting ___ in
1.
Gtrs. 4 & 5: w/ Rhy. Fills 1 & 1A
A
G D
2.
___ real - ly can't re - sist.
such a stick - y

Bridge

Gtr. 2 tacet

Lyrics: mess. If I say a word, just stop me 'cause I real- ly should shut up. Guess I'll split now. Just for- get

*Gtrs. 1, 5 & 6
*Composite arrangement; Gtr. 6 (acous.), played *mf*.

**Gtr. 7
f w/ dist.   P.M.

**Bass arr. for gtr.
***Chord symbols reflect implied harmony.

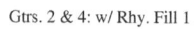

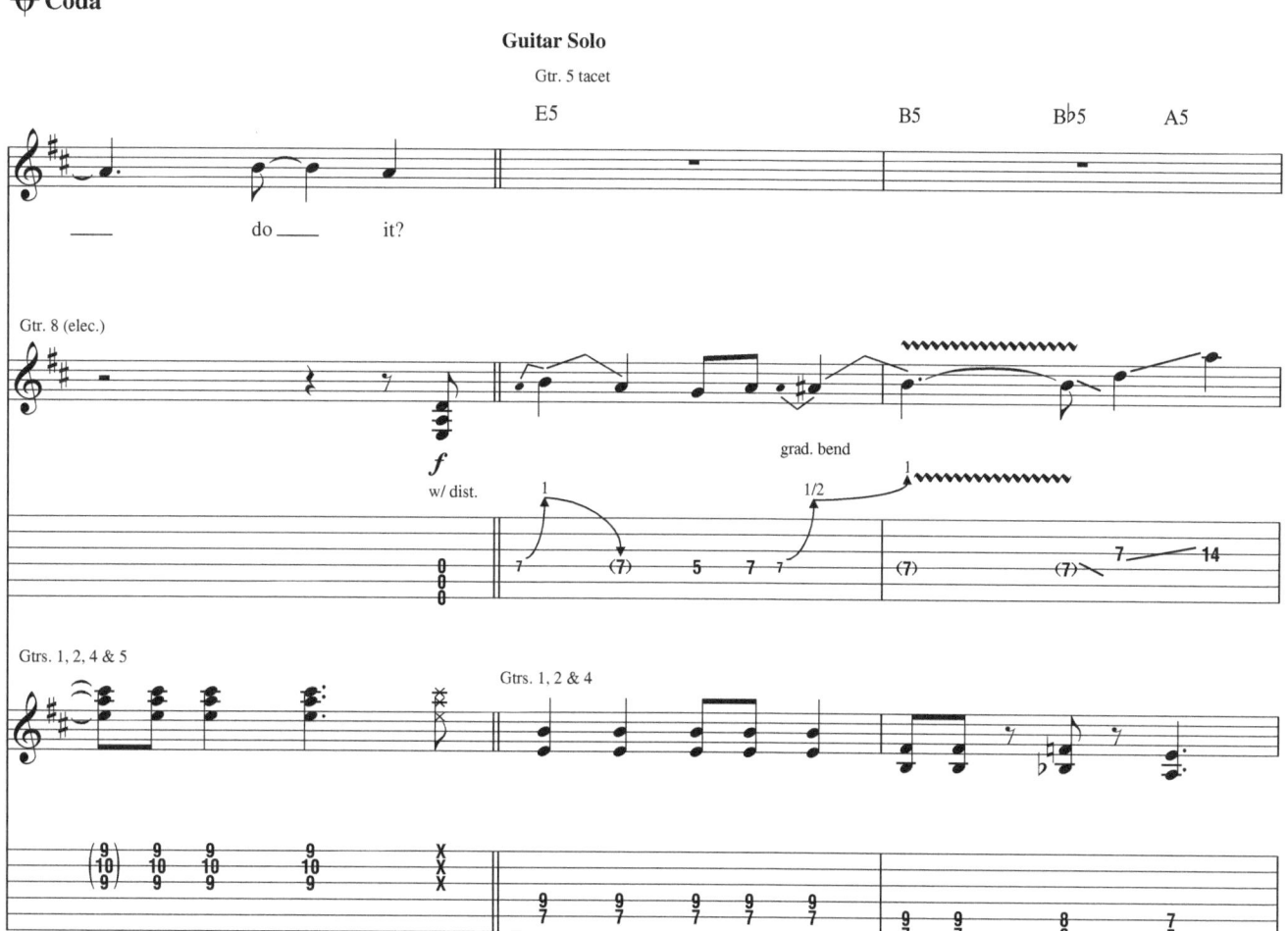

D.S. al Coda

Coda

Guitar Solo

E5
B5
B♭5
A5
D5
A5
A♭5
G5
D5
P.H.
hold bend
Pitch: B C♯
A5
A♭5
G5
E5
B5
B♭5
A5
E5
let ring
let ring
let ring

B5
B♭5
A5
D5
A5
A♭5
G5
D5
8va
*2nd str. caught with previous bend.
Verse
Gtrs. 1, 2 & 4 tacet
E5
D
3. Hey, girl, now walk
loco
steady gliss.
Gtrs. 5 & 6
let ring

me home. No, drive me home. Now pick me up a - gain.

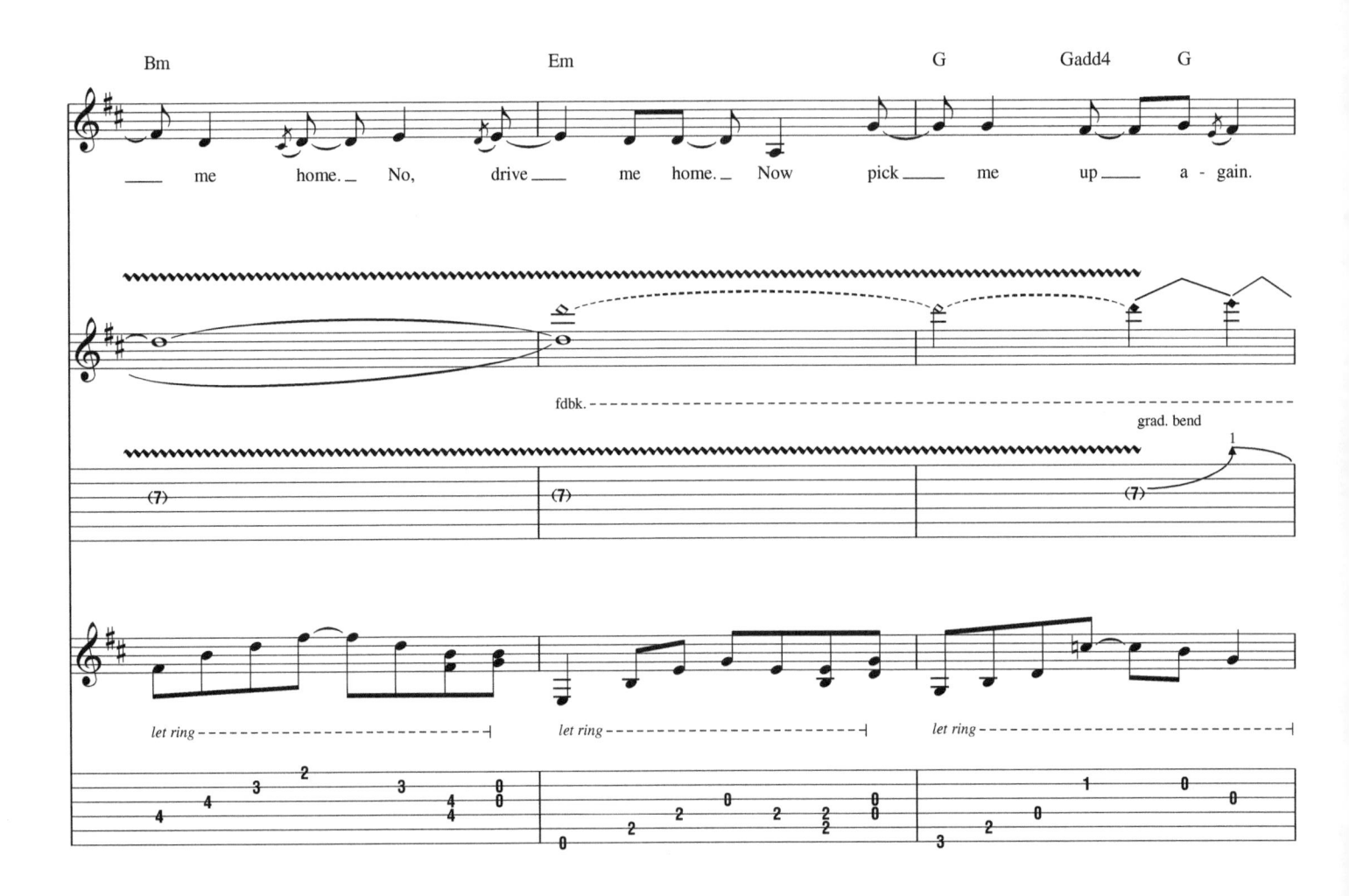

Wait - ing for things to change, I'll re - ar - range stuff. No,

Bridge
G Gadd4 G A Asus4 A
not you a - gain. If I say a word, just stop
grad. bend
let ring
G Gadd4 G Gadd4 G A Asus4
me 'cause I real - ly should shut up. Guess I'll
w/ bar
let ring

split now. Just forget you met me. Sorry I fucked it all up.

Outro

A tempo

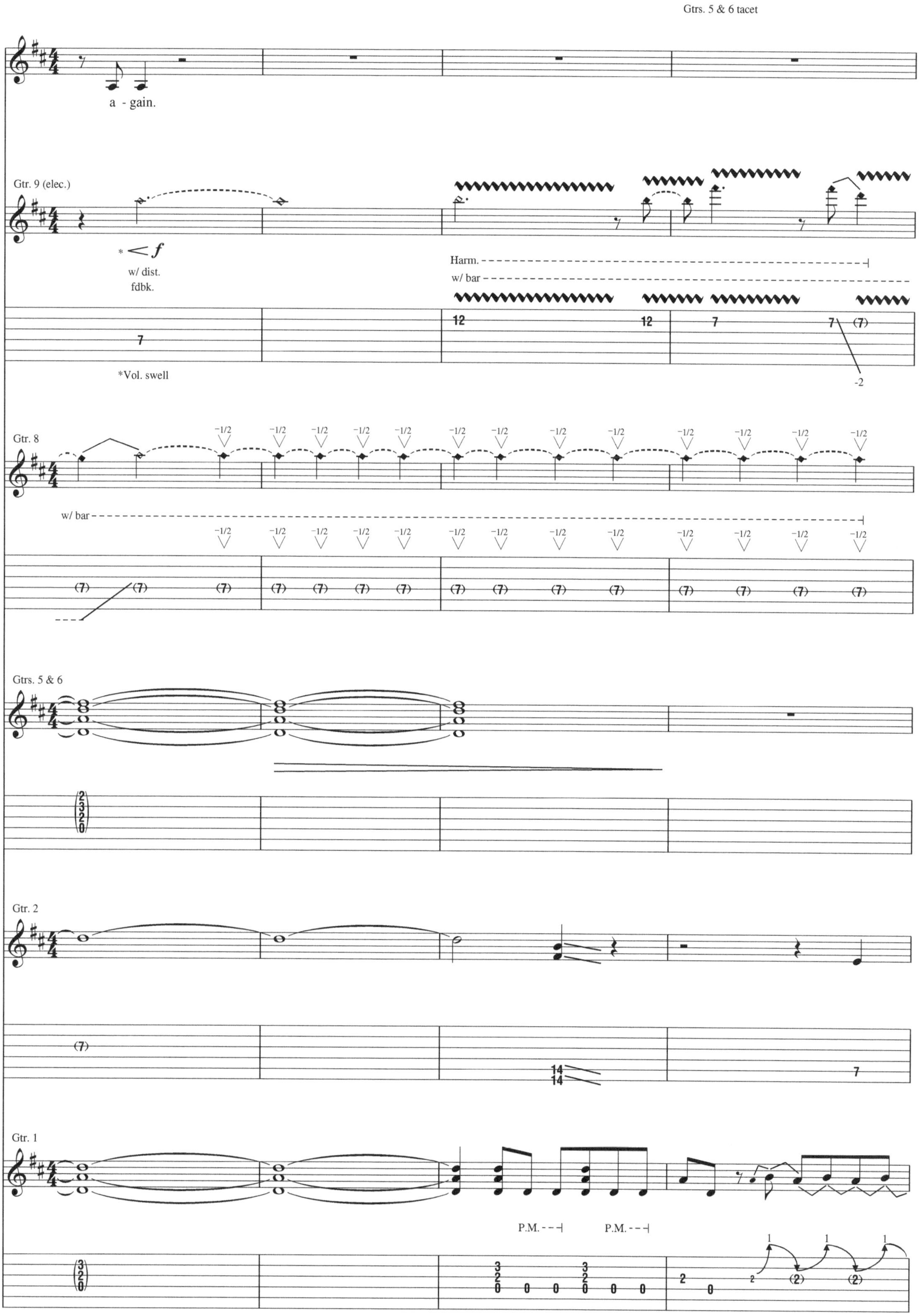

Begin fade
Gtr. 2 tacet
N.C.
15ma
Gtr. 9
P.H.
w/ bar
Pitch: E
B
Gtr. 8
w/ bar
Gtr. 2
Gtr. 1
Fade out
Gtr. 9 tacet
Gtr. 8
P.H.
w/ bar
Gtr. 1
let ring

from *Where You Been*

Out There

Words and Music by J Mascis

Gtrs. 1 & 3: Capo III

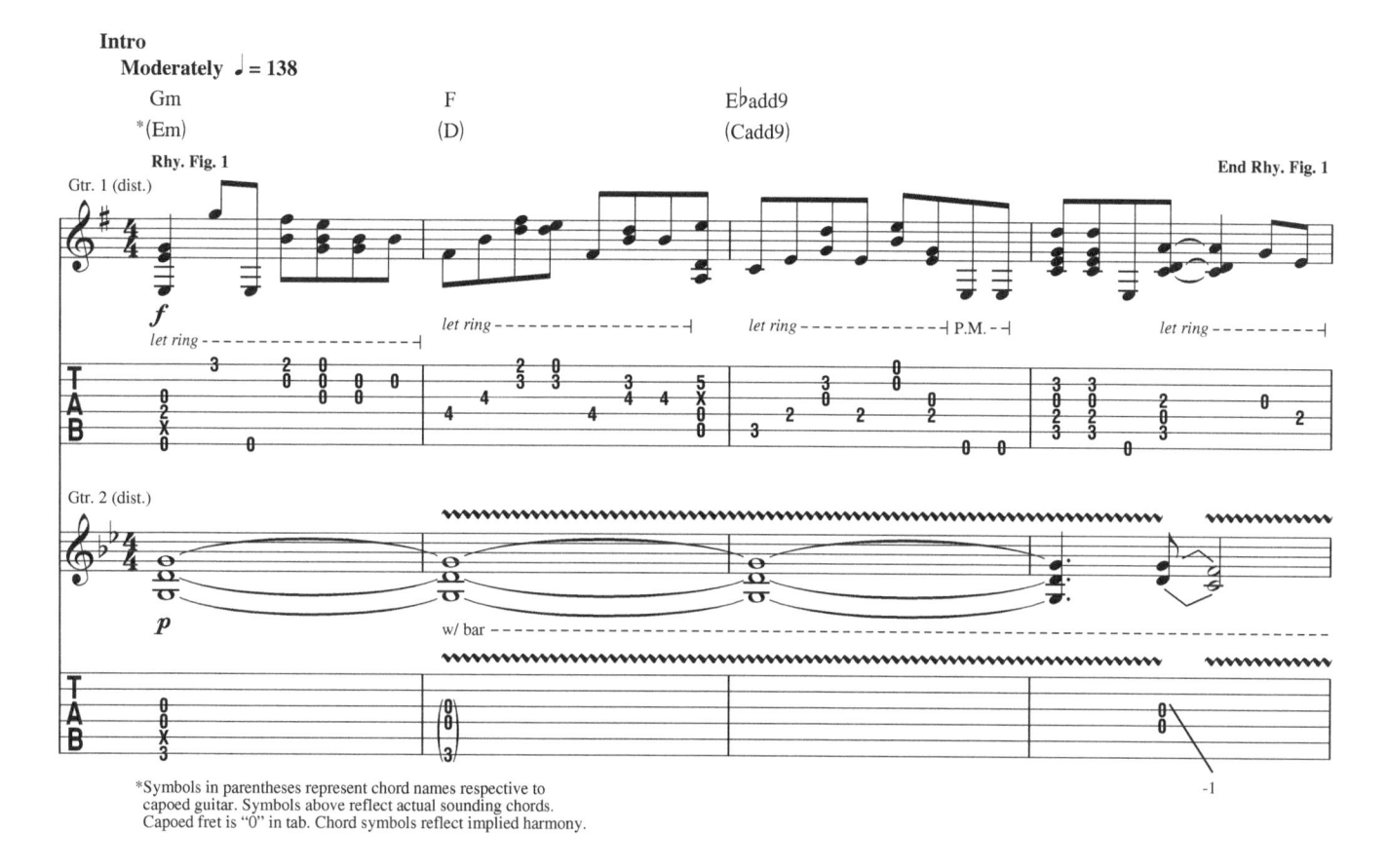

Intro
Moderately ♩ = 138

*Symbols in parentheses represent chord names respective to capoed guitar. Symbols above reflect actual sounding chords. Capoed fret is "0" in tab. Chord symbols reflect implied harmony.

**Gtrs. 1 & 3: w/ Rhy. Fig. 1 (4 times)

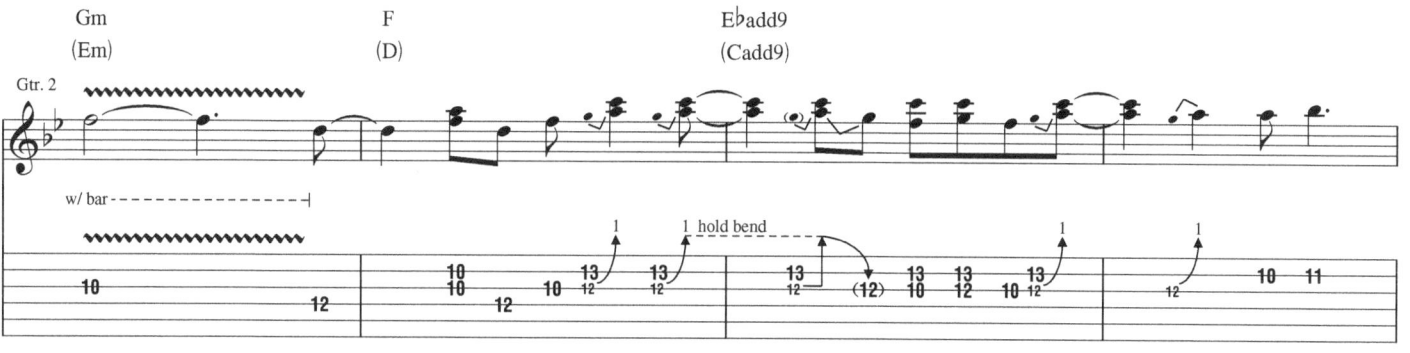

**Gtr. 3 (dist.), played *ff*.

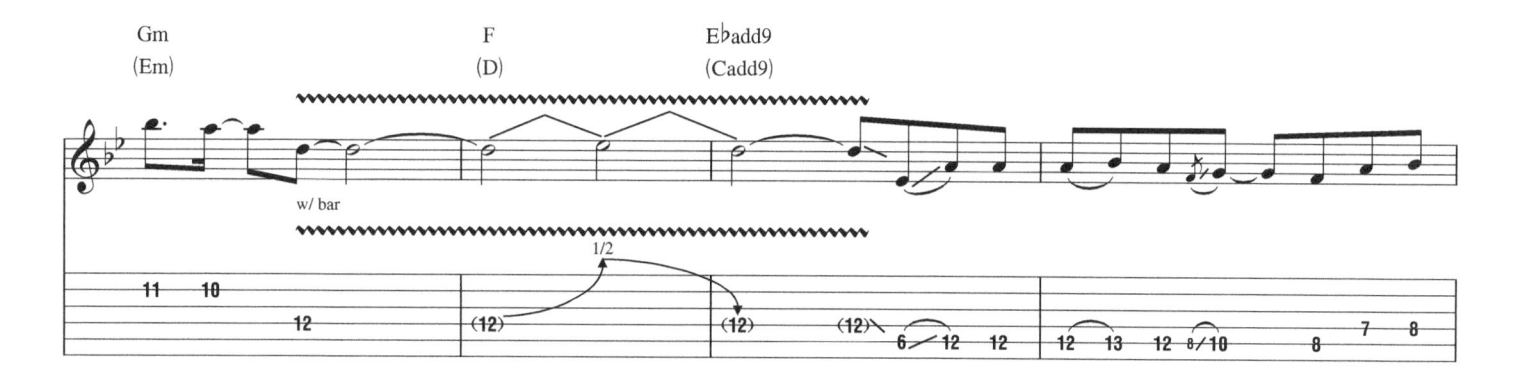

Copyright © 1993 Spam As The Bread Music
All Rights Administered by Chrysalis Songs
All Rights Reserved   Used by Permission

63

Gm (Em) F (D) E♭add9 (Cadd9)
Gm (Em) F (D) E♭add9 (Cadd9)
Gm (Em)
Gtr. 2
w/ bar
let ring
Gtrs. 1 & 3
let ring
𝄋 Verse
Gtrs. 1 & 3: w/ Rhy. Fig. 1 (4 times)
Gtr. 2 tacet
Gm (Em) F (D) E♭add9 (Cadd9)
1. I know your name.
3. I know it's sick.

Gm (Em) F (D) E♭add9 (Cadd9)
I know the peo - ple out there feel the same.
I know you think a - gain it's just a trick.
Gm (Em) F (D) E♭add9 (Cadd9)
I know you're gone.
May - be I've changed.
To Coda
Gm (Em) F (D) E♭add9 (Cadd9)
I hope you got some friends to come a - long.
Just tell me, was this all in vain?
Gtr. 2
w/ slide
steady gliss.
Chorus
F (D) E♭maj7 (Cmaj7)
I know you're out there.
Gtr. 2
steady gliss.
Rhy. Fig. 2
Gtrs. 1 & 3

Lyrics:
I know you're gone.
You can't say that's fair.

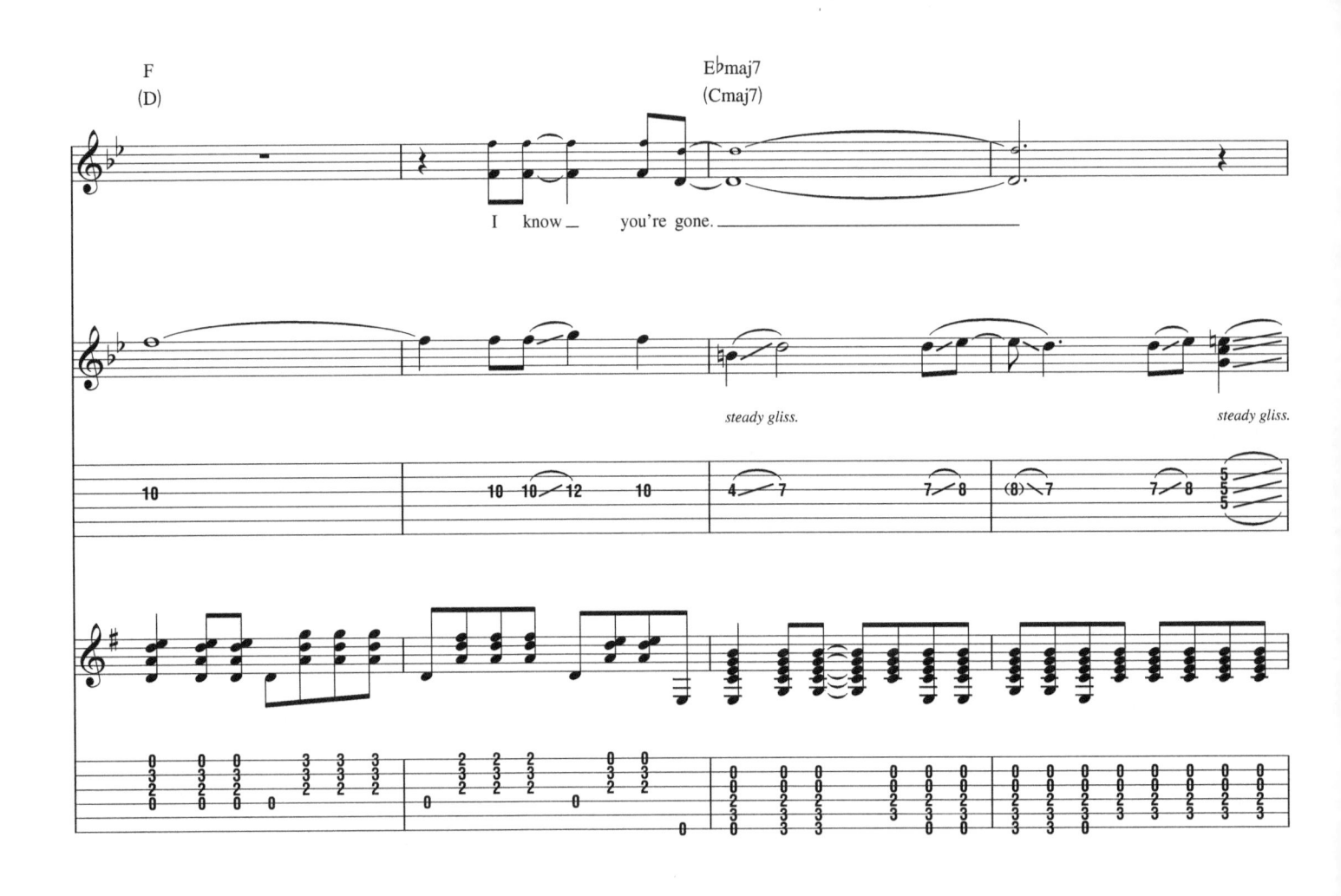

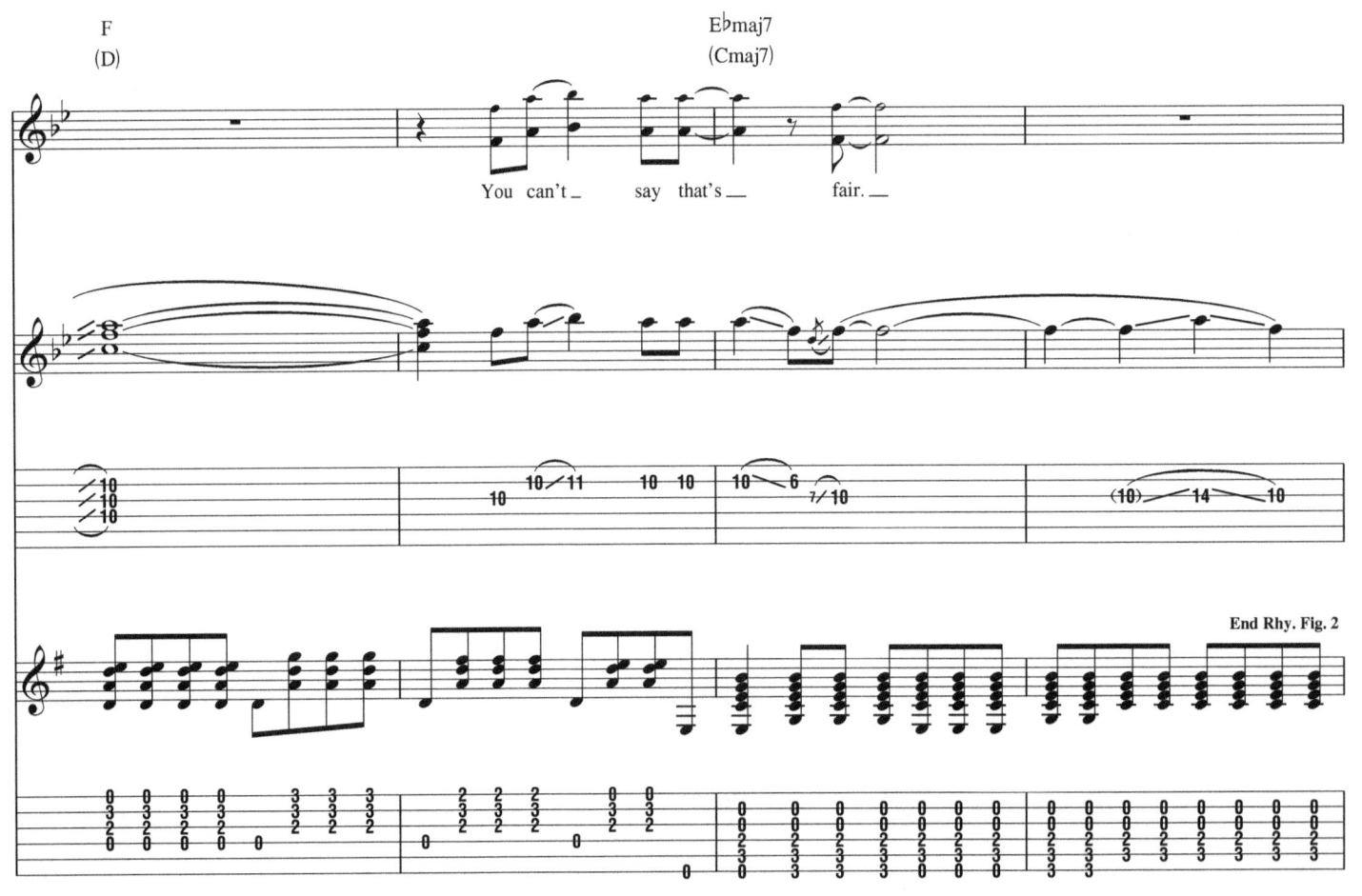

67

Verse

Lyrics:
- Can't you be wrong?
- 2. I feel O.K.
- Sure, I know that's not what people say.

Chords: F (D), Ebmaj7 (Cmaj7), Gm (Em), F (D), Ebadd9 (Cadd9)

Gtrs. 1 & 3: w/ Rhy. Fig. 1 (4 times)
End Rhy. Fig. 2
Gtr. 2, w/o slide

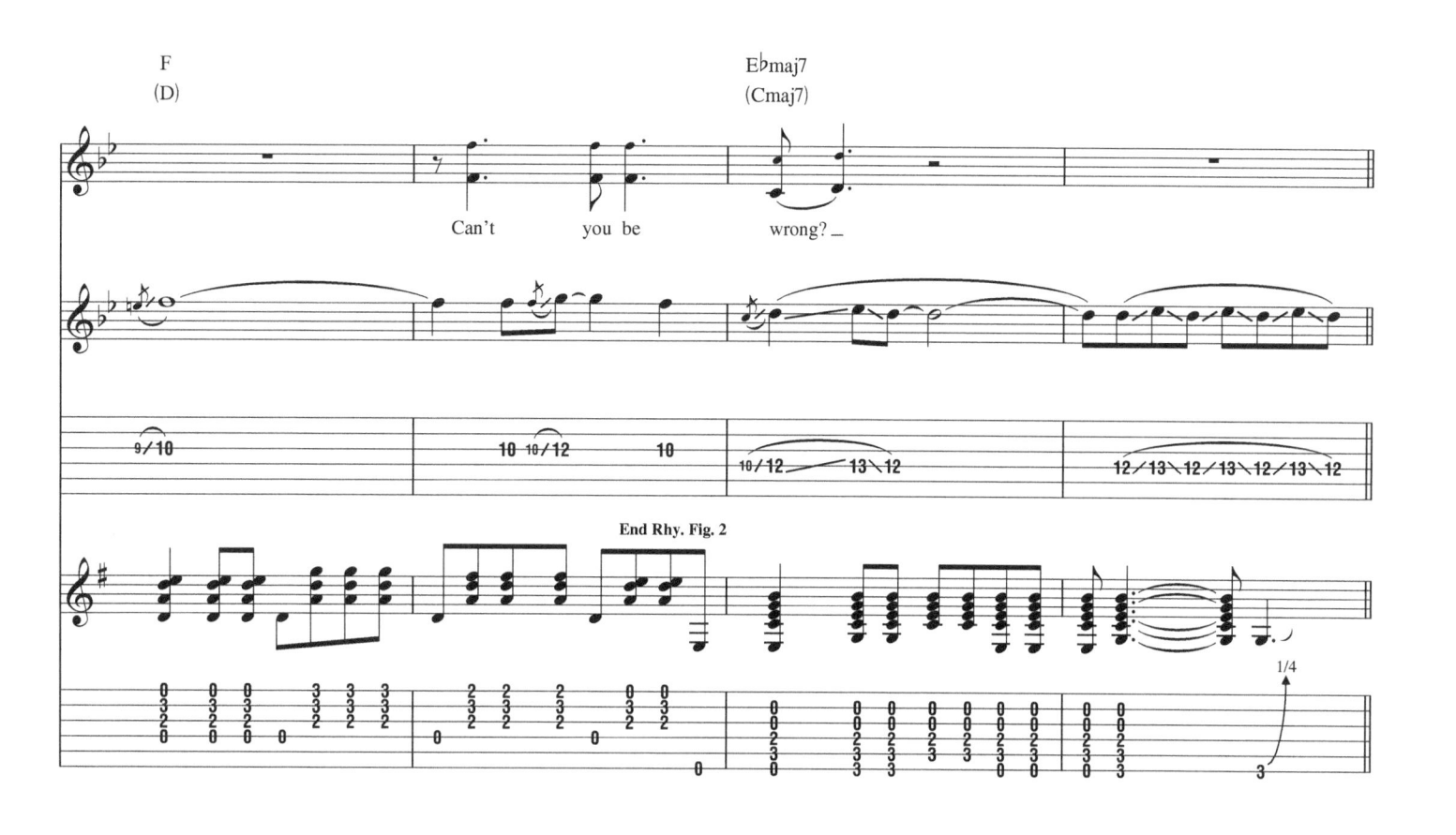

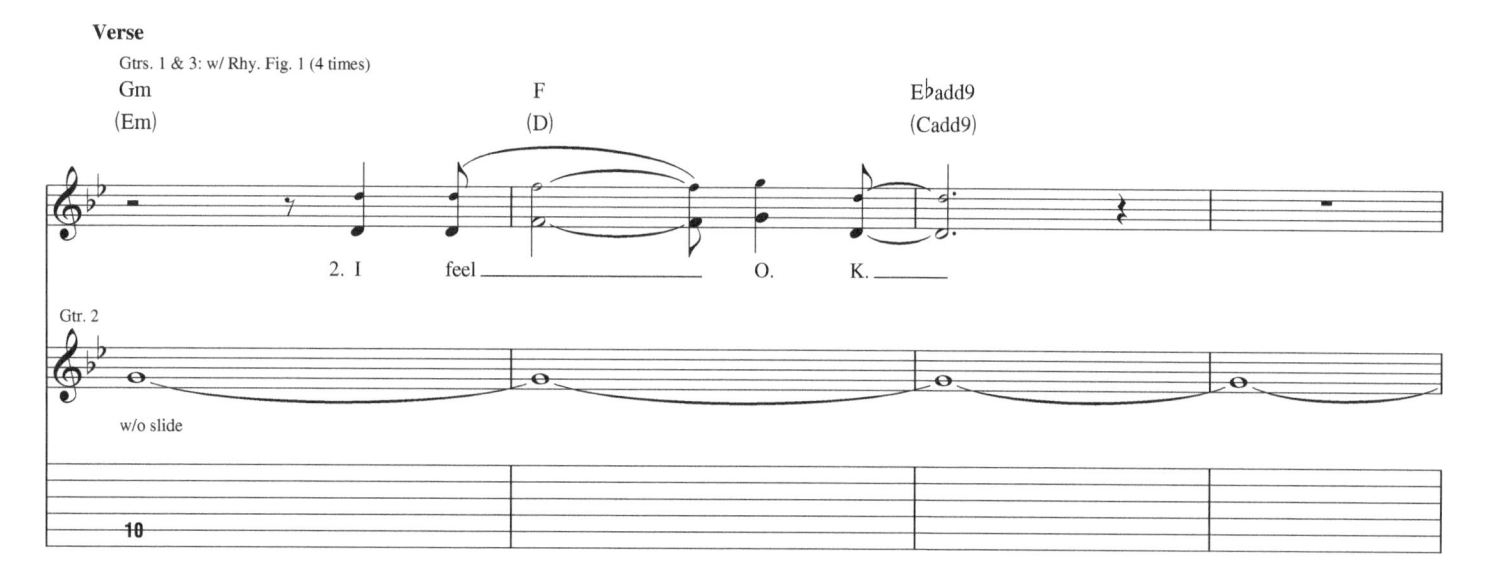

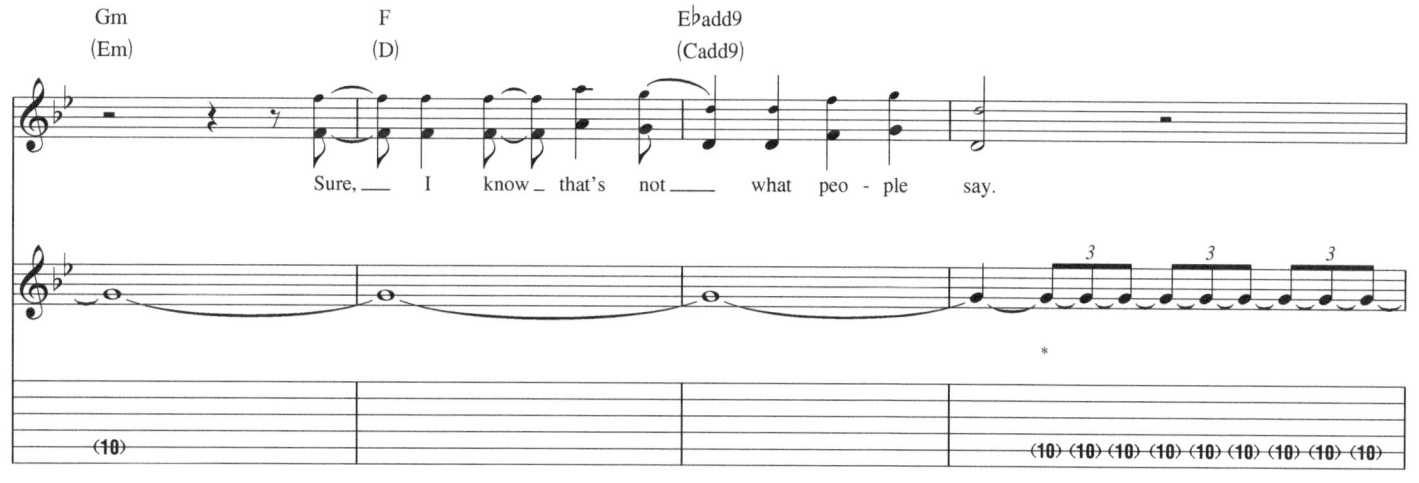

*Using a guitar with Les Paul-style electronics, set the lead volume to 0 and the rhythm volume to 10. Flip the pickup selector switch in the rhythm indicated to simulate the re-attack.

Gm (Em) F (D) E♭add9 (Cadd9)

May - be they're wrong?

Gm (Em) F (D) E♭add9 (Cadd9)

May - be you weren't on my side all a - long?

w/ slide
steady gliss.

Chorus
Gtrs. 1 & 3: w/ Rhy. Fig. 2

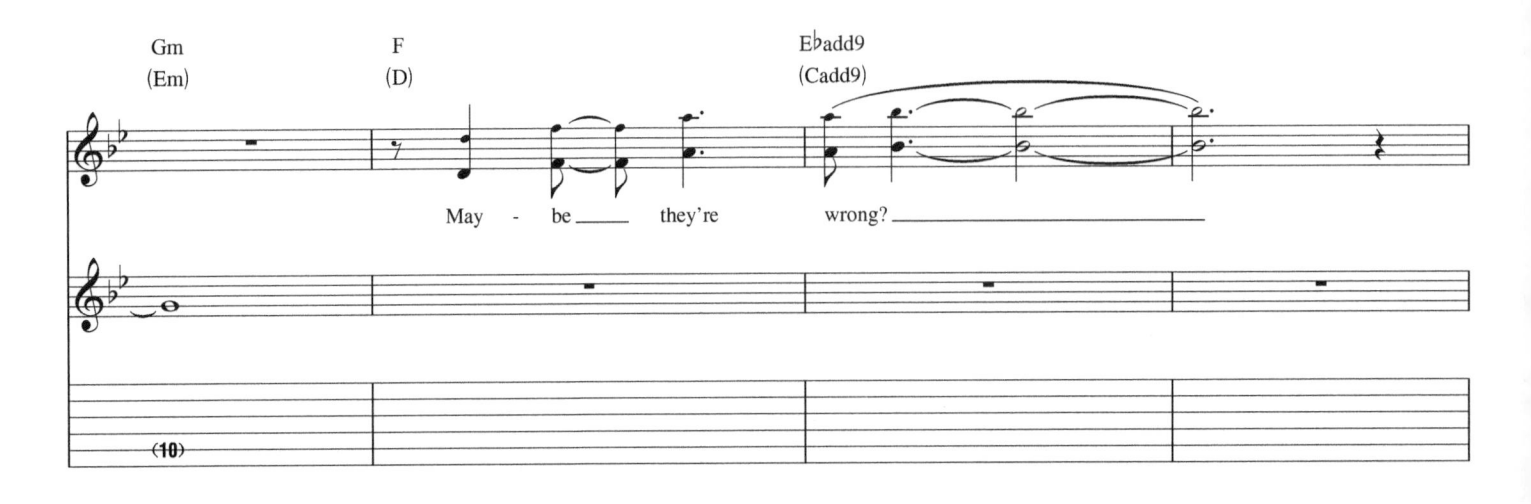

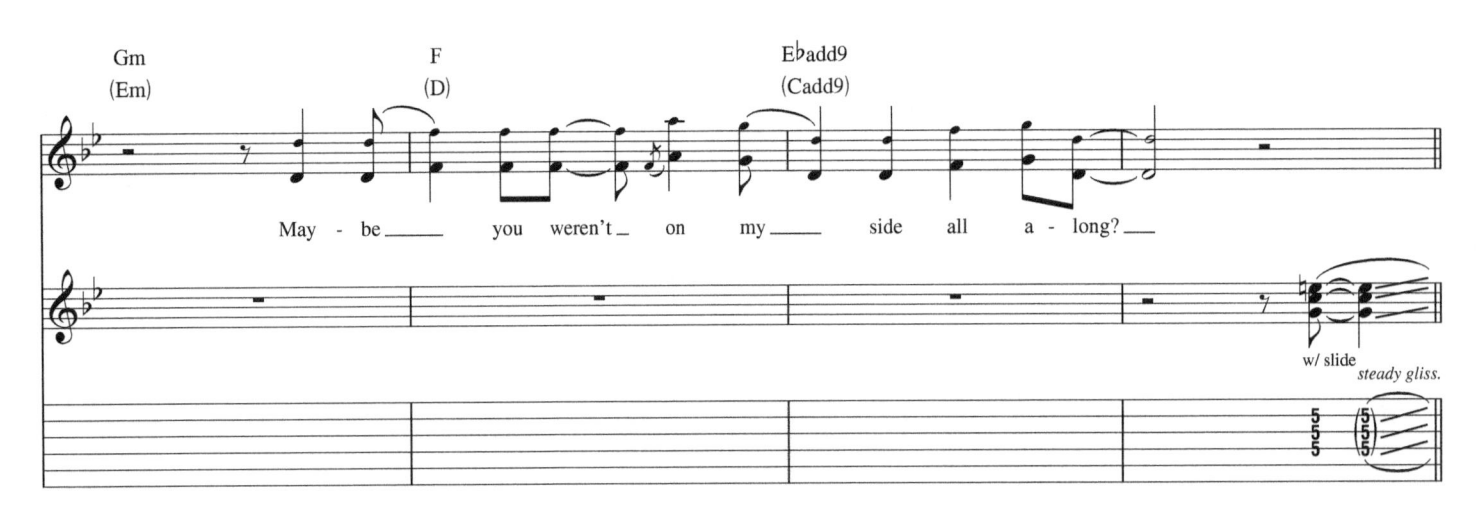

F (D) E♭maj7 (Cmaj7)

I know you're out there.

steady gliss.

F (D) E♭maj7 (Cmaj7)

I know you're gone.

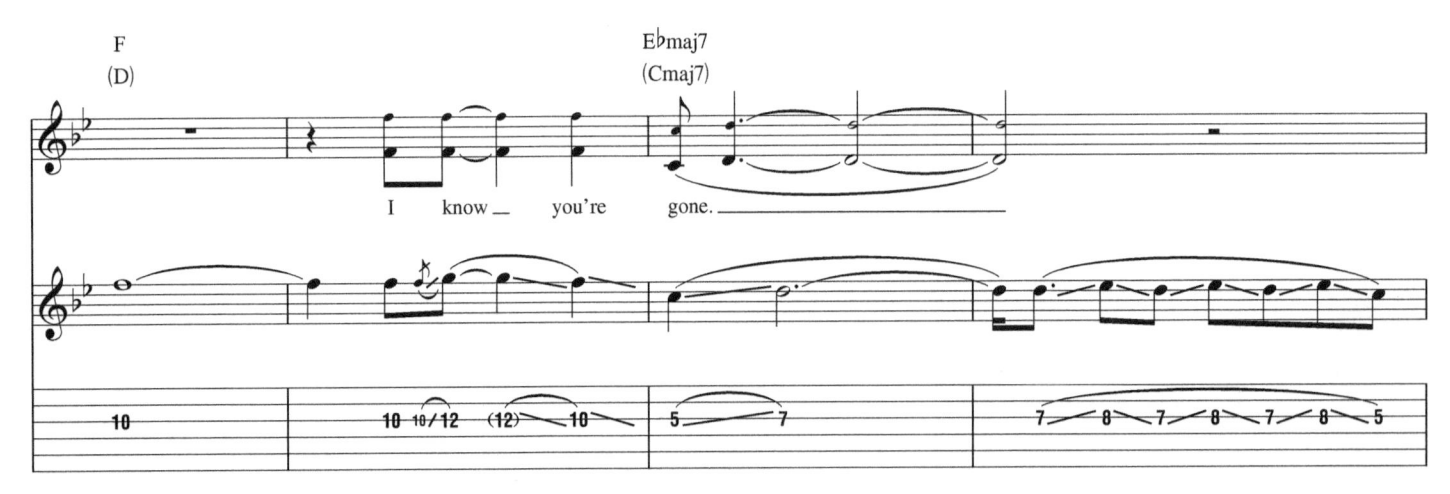

68

Bridge

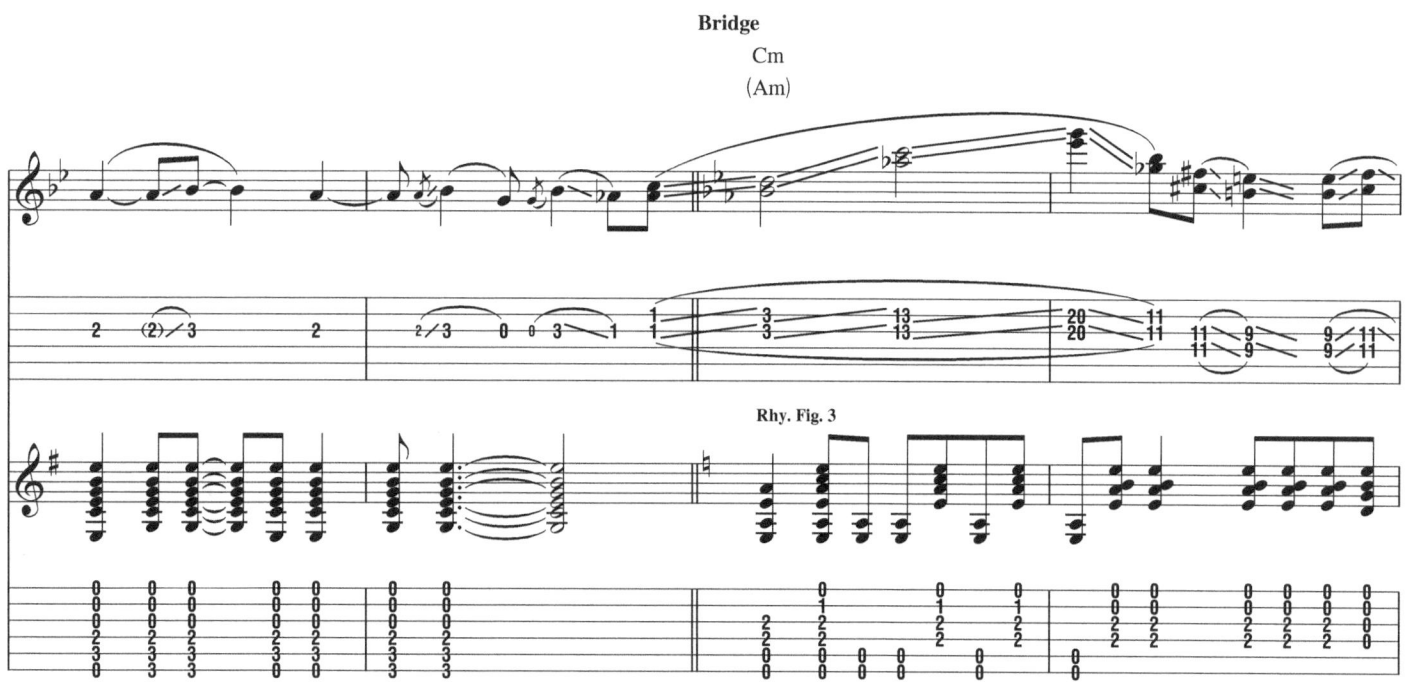

69

E♭maj7
(Cmaj7)
I know you're out there, you're still a case,
P.M.
Gtr. 2 tacet
A♭add9
(Fadd9)
Cm
(Am)
it's still the place, weren't you in - vit - ed?
End Rhy. Fig. 3
Gtrs. 1 & 3
*T
*T = Thumb on 6th string
E♭maj7
(Cmaj7)
It's what you can't spare, what-ev-er's left,

just hide the rest, and bring it right in.

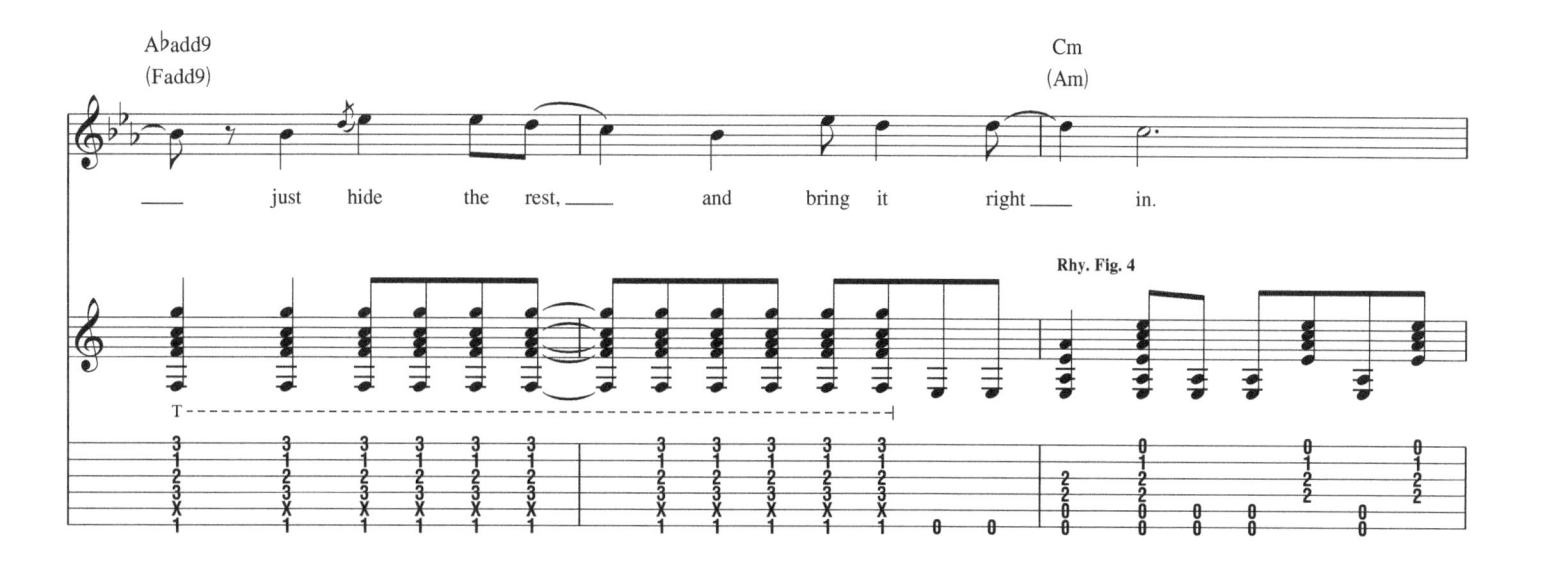

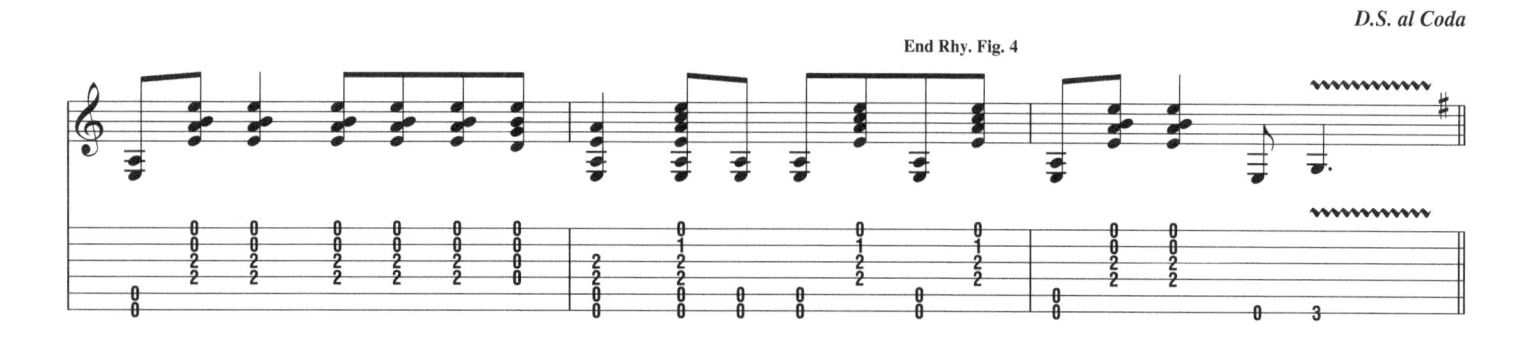

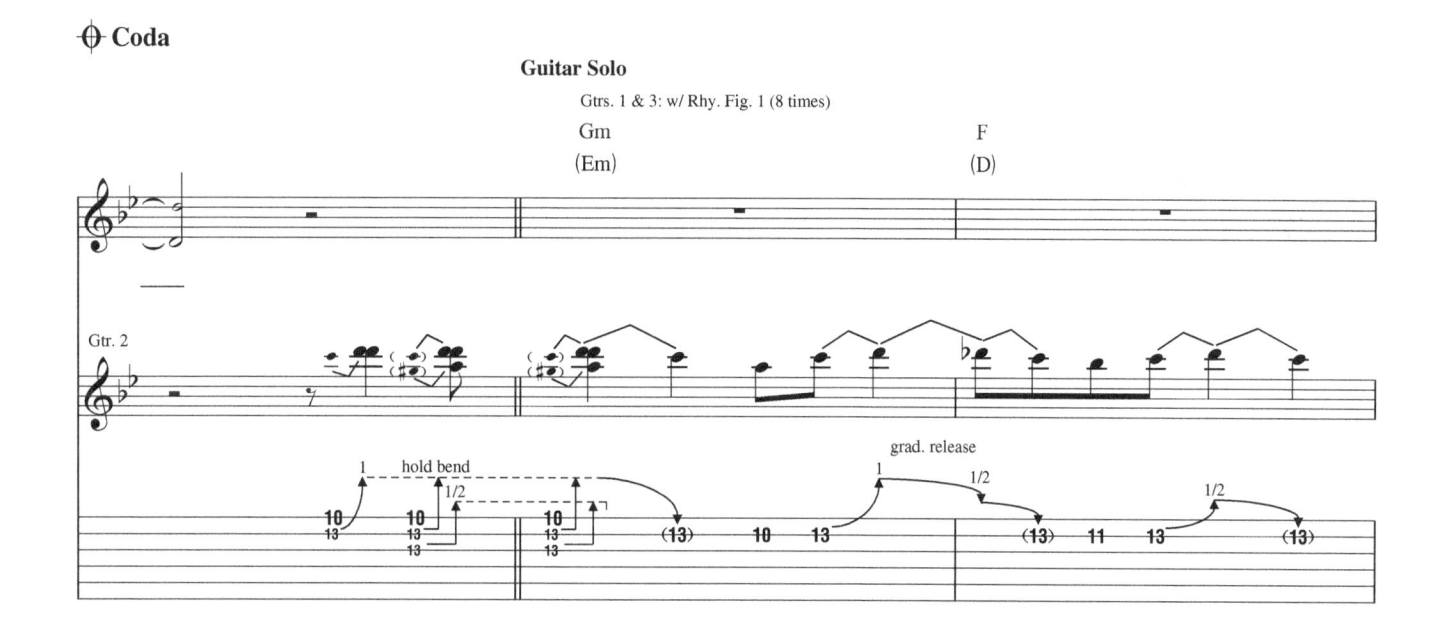

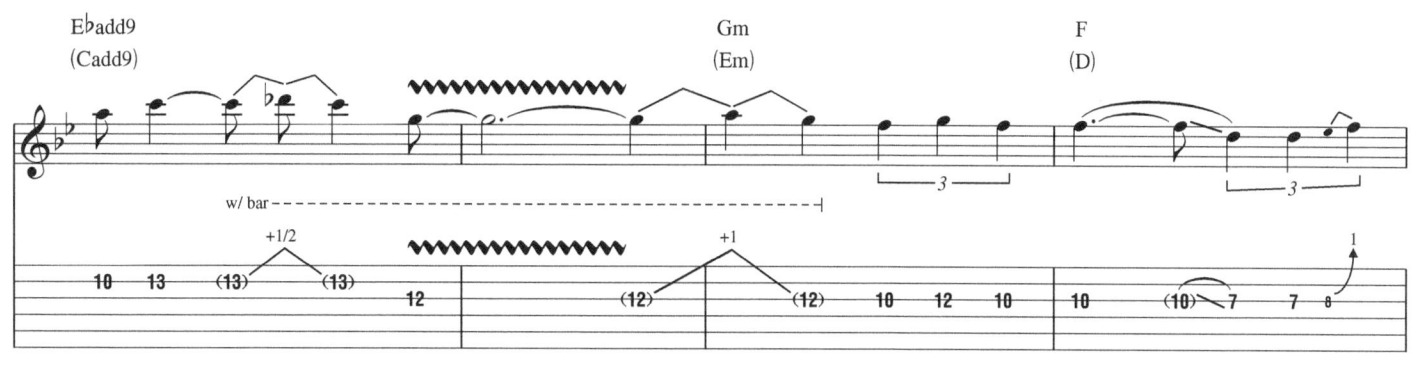

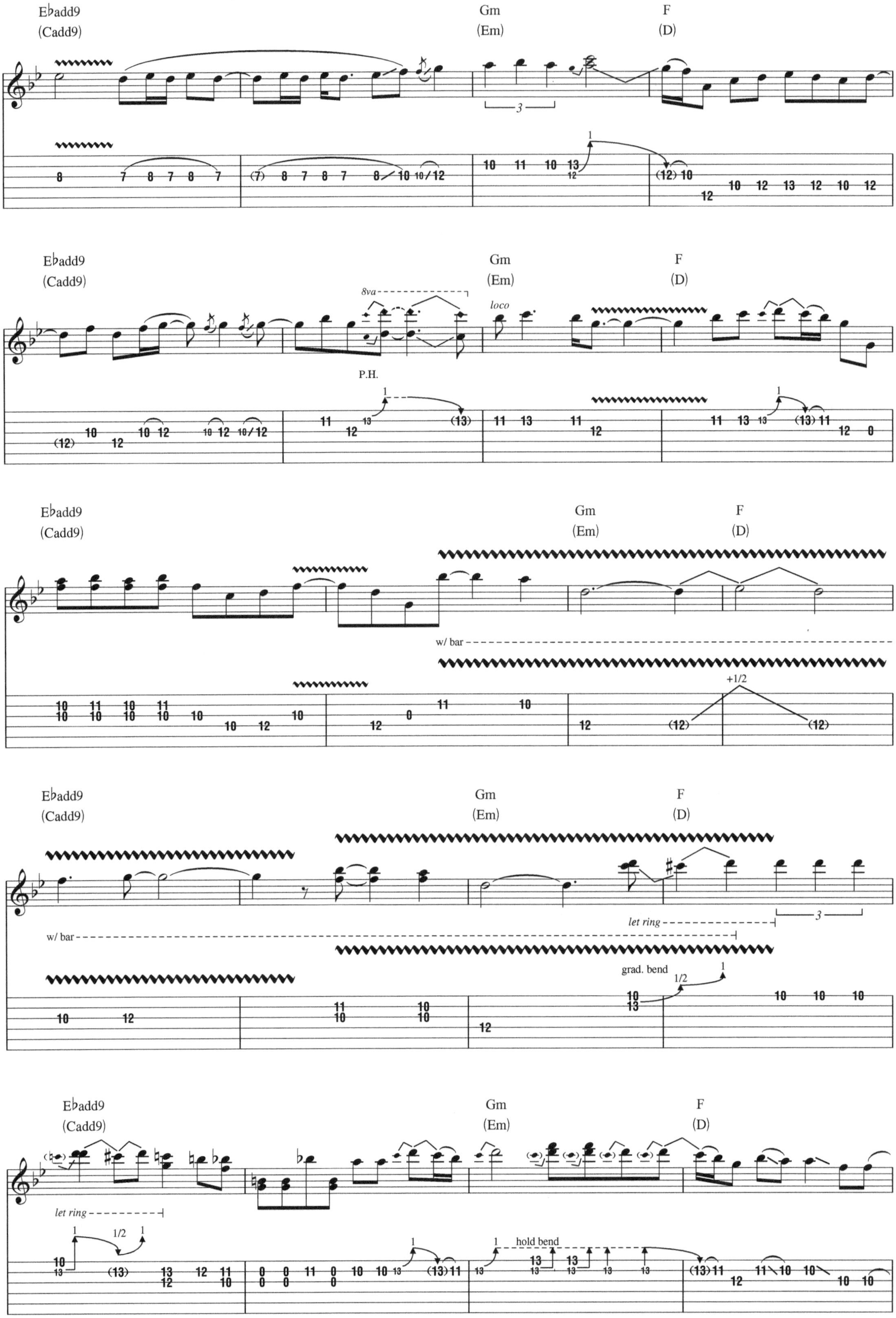
E♭add9
(Cadd9)
Gm
(Em)
F
(D)
8va
P.H.
loco
w/ bar
let ring
grad. bend
hold bend

Bridge

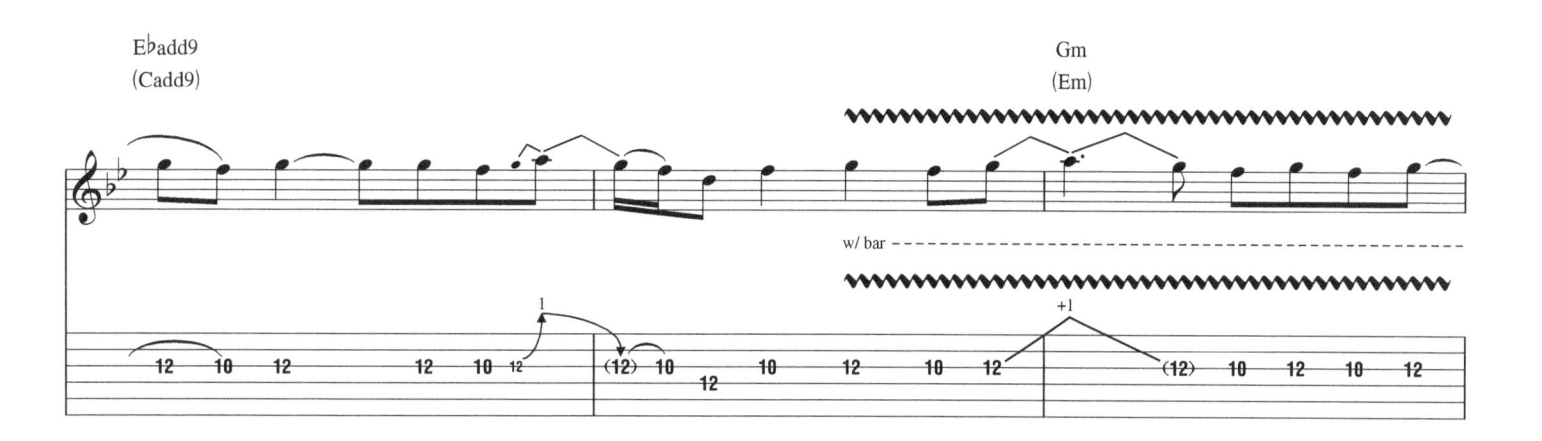

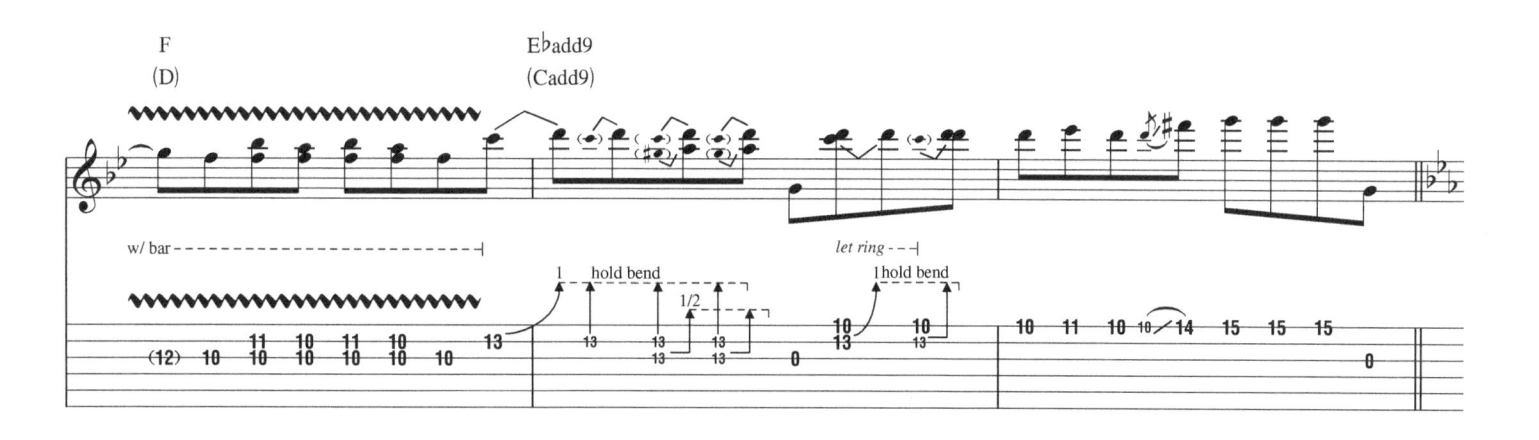

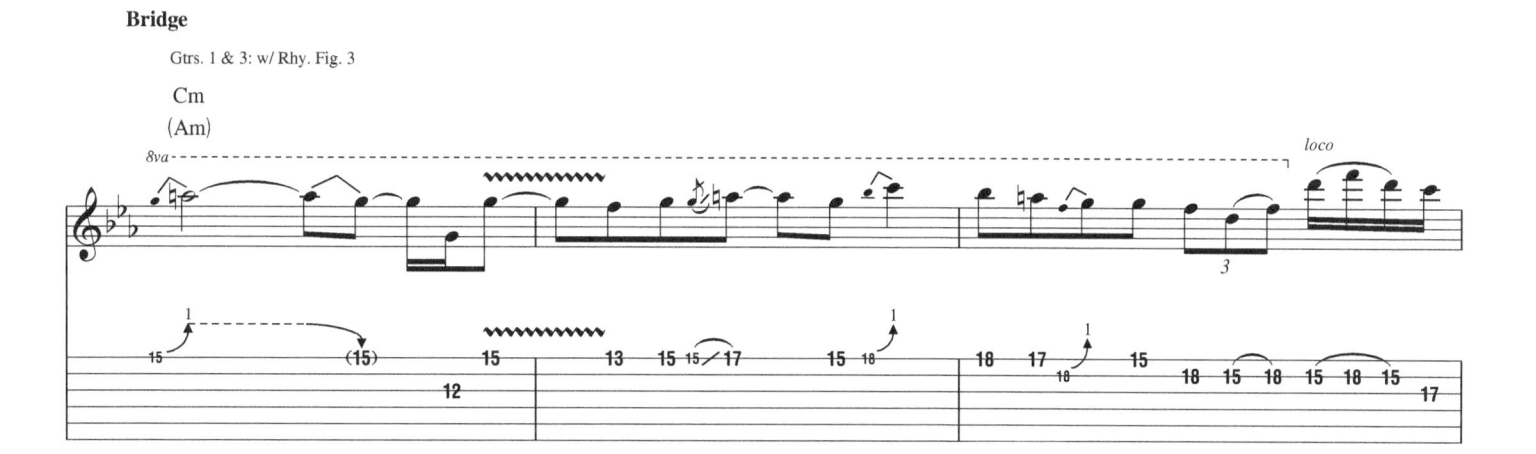

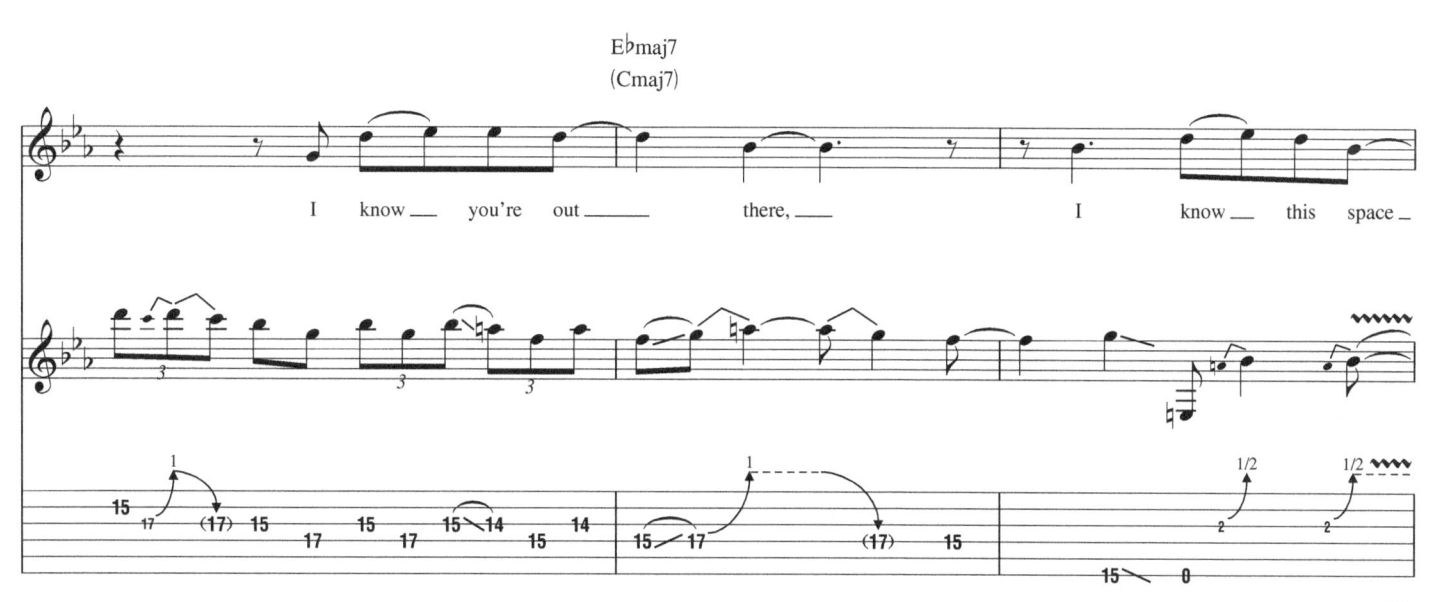

I know you're out there, I know this space

A♭add9
(Fadd9)
Cm
(Am)
is not a race, weren't you in - vit - ed?
let ring
E♭maj7
(Cmaj7)
It's what you can't spare,
A♭add9
(Fadd9)
what - ev - er's left, just hide the rest and bring it right
Cm
(Am)
in.

75

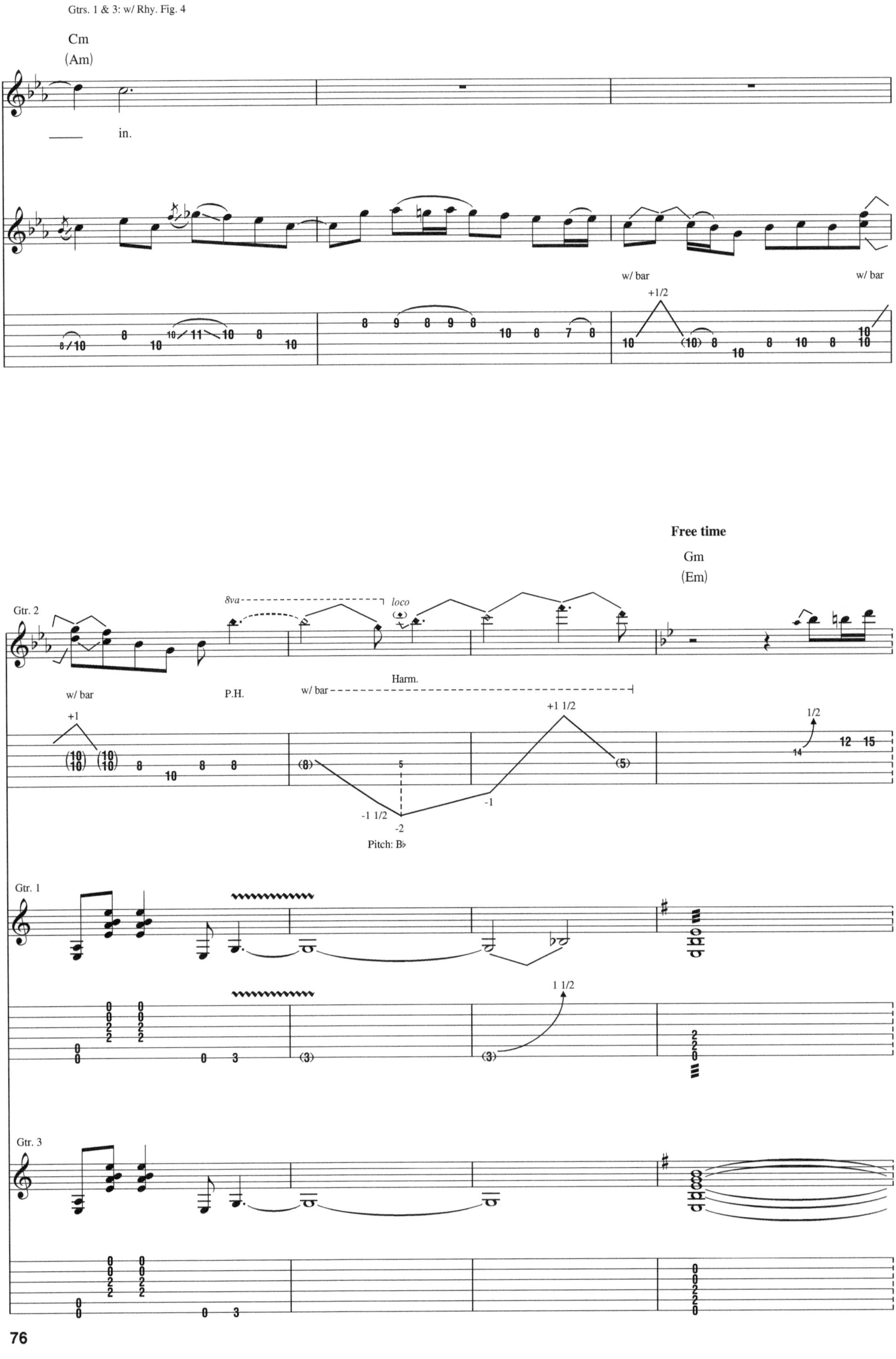
Gtrs. 1 & 3: w/ Rhy. Fig. 4
Cm
(Am)
in.
w/ bar
+1/2
w/ bar
Free time
Gm
(Em)
Gtr. 2
8va
loco
w/ bar
+1
P.H.
Harm.
w/ bar
+1 1/2
1/2
-1 1/2
-2
-1
Pitch: B♭
Gtr. 1
1 1/2
Gtr. 3

77

from *You're Living All Over Me*

Raisans
Words and Music by J Mascis

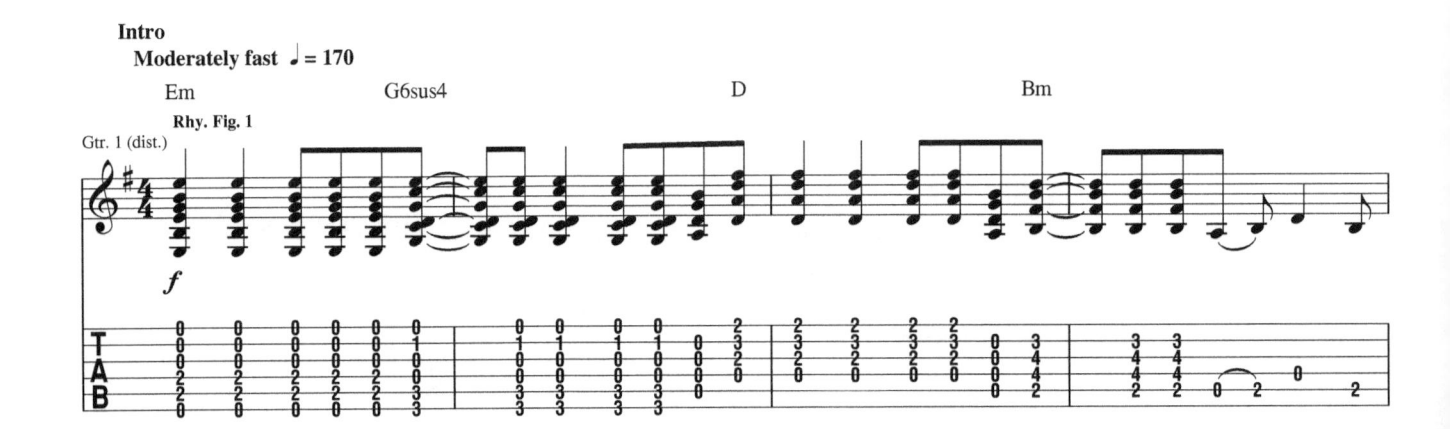

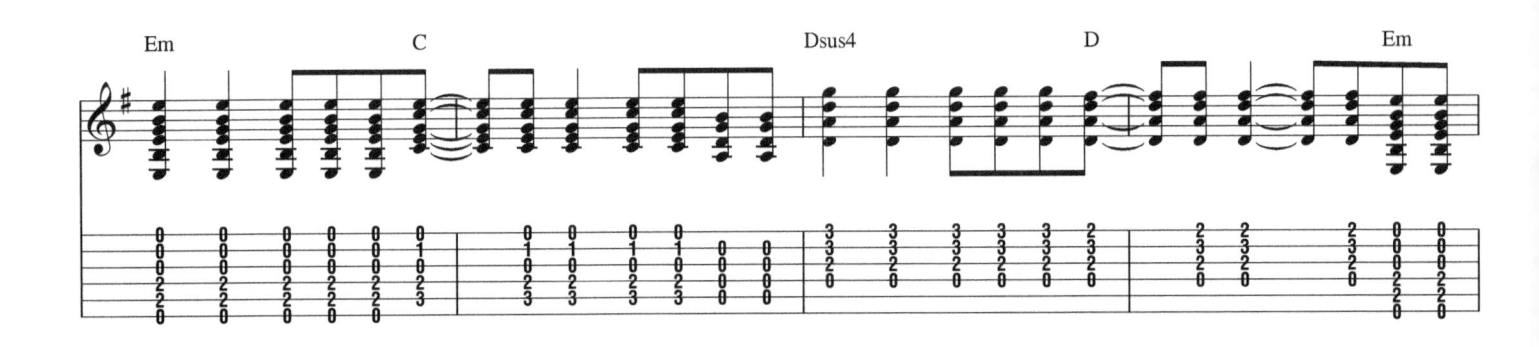

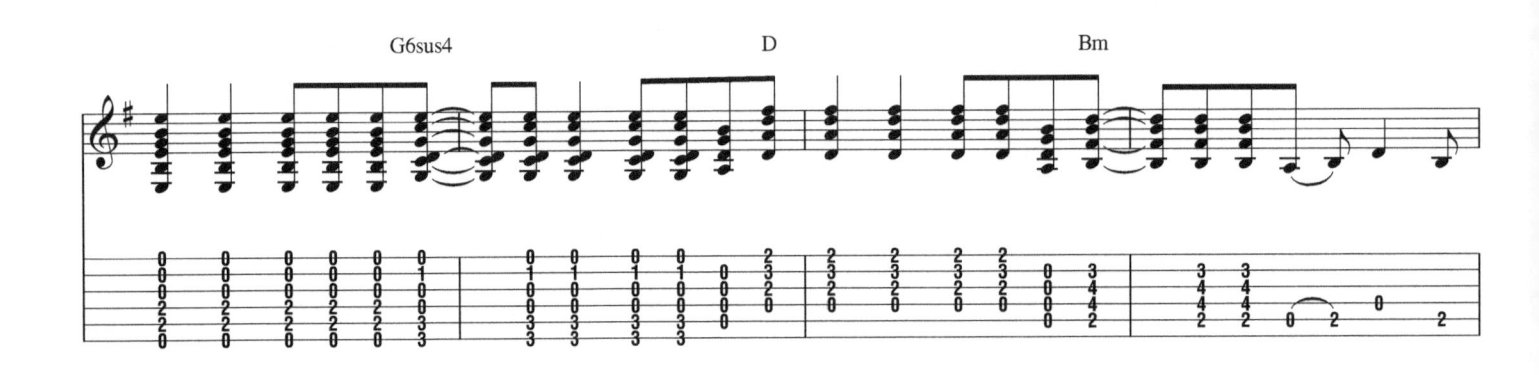

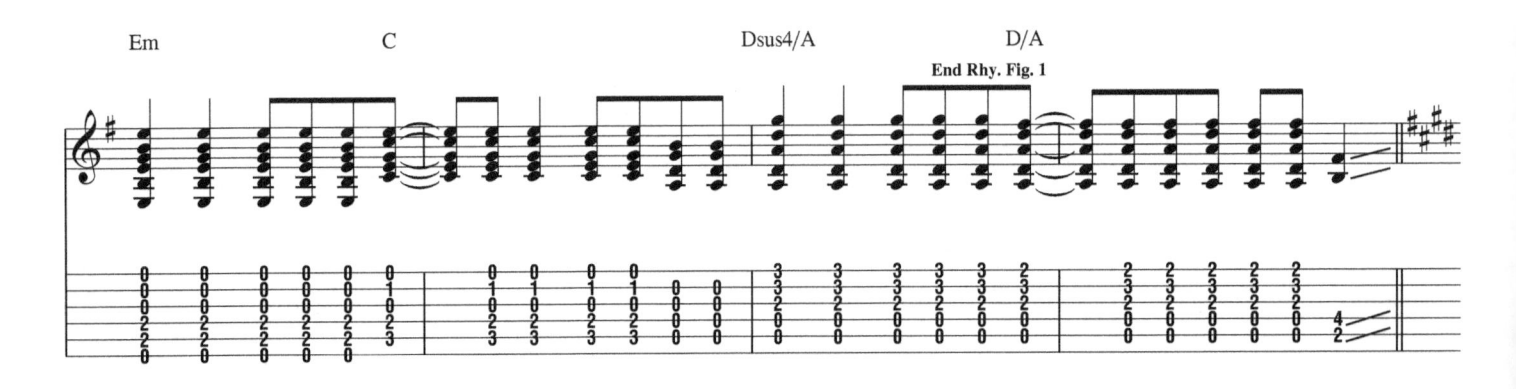

Verse

1. The lights exploded, she stood burning in front of me.

She ripped my heart out and gave it to me.

My eyes wouldn't open cemented to her face.

Have I begun a feeble chase?

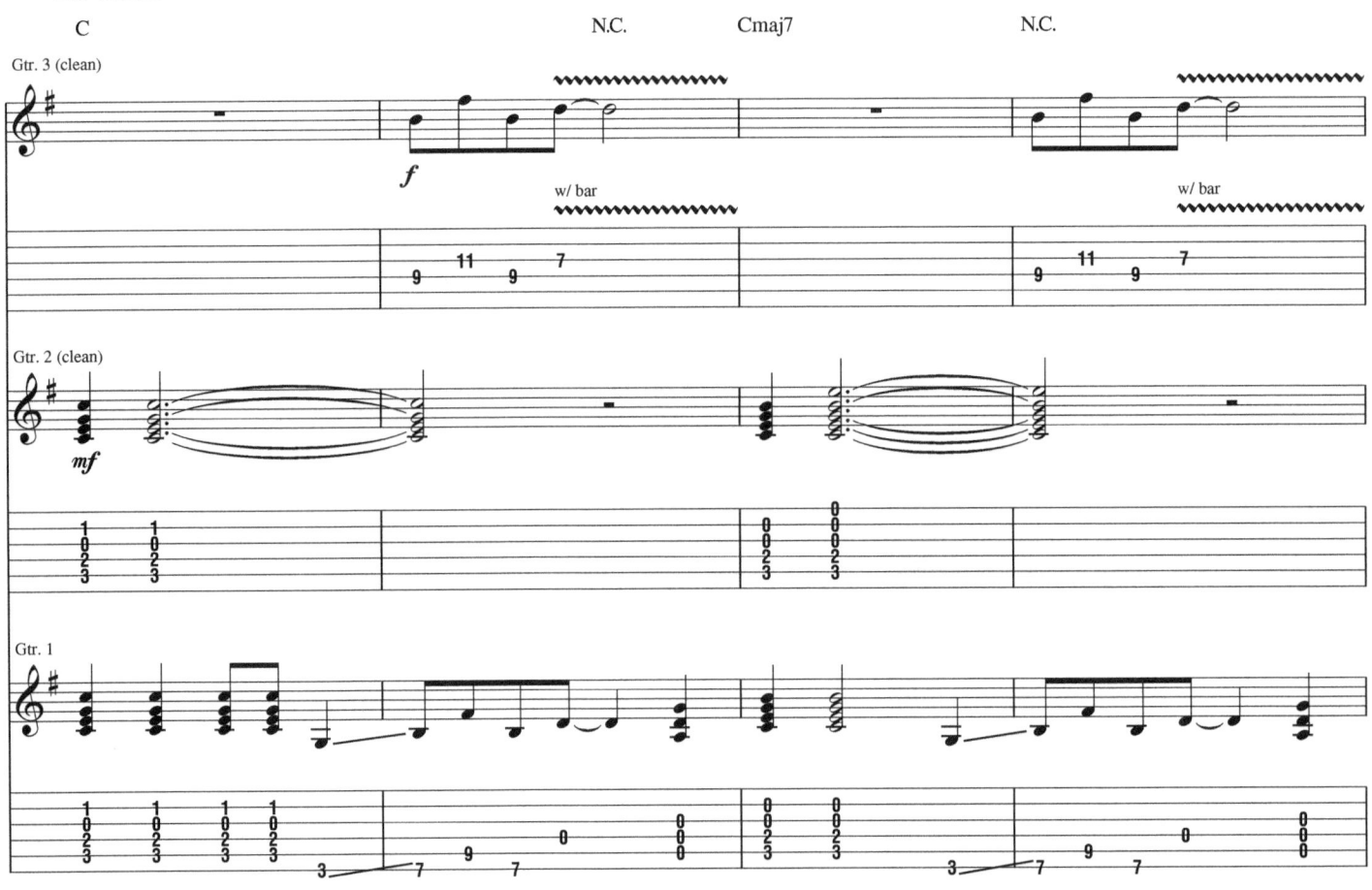

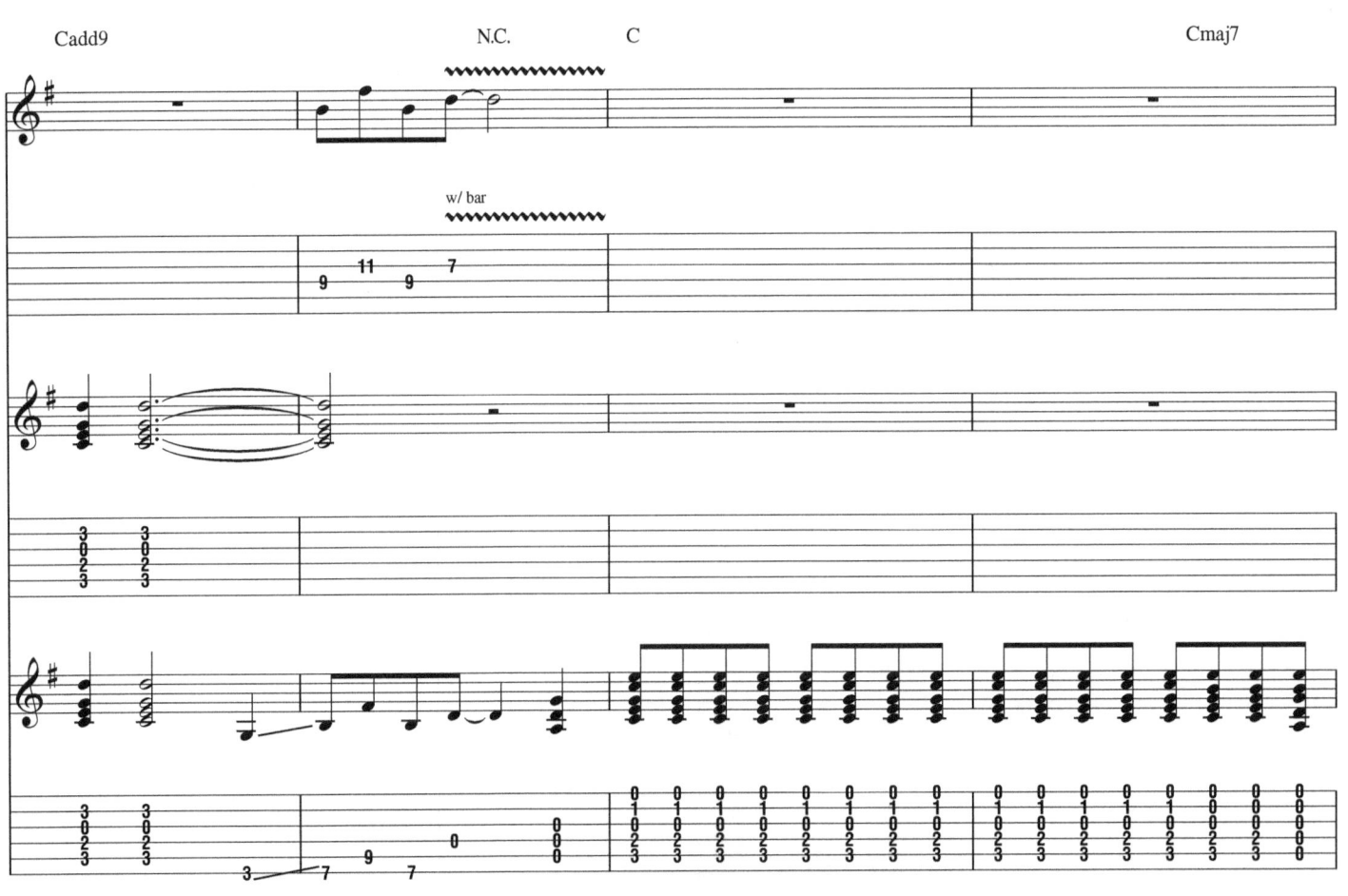

Pre-Chorus

Em7
Gtr. 3: w/ Fill 1
N.C.(D)
P.S.
Chorus
Gtr. 1: w/ Rhy. Fig. 1
2nd time, Gtrs. 2 & 3 tacet
3rd time, Gtr. 5 tacet
Em G6sus4 D Bm
I'll be down. I'll be a - round,
* Voc. doubled next 8 meas., 3rd time only.
To Coda 2
Em C Dsus4 D
I'll be hang - ing where e - ven - tual - ly you'll have to be.
Em G6sus4 D Bm
I'll just stare, and hope you'll care.
To Coda 1
Em C Dsus4/A D/A
It's on - ly ev - 'ry - thing stand - ing in front of
Fill 1
Gtr. 3
w/ bar
slack

82

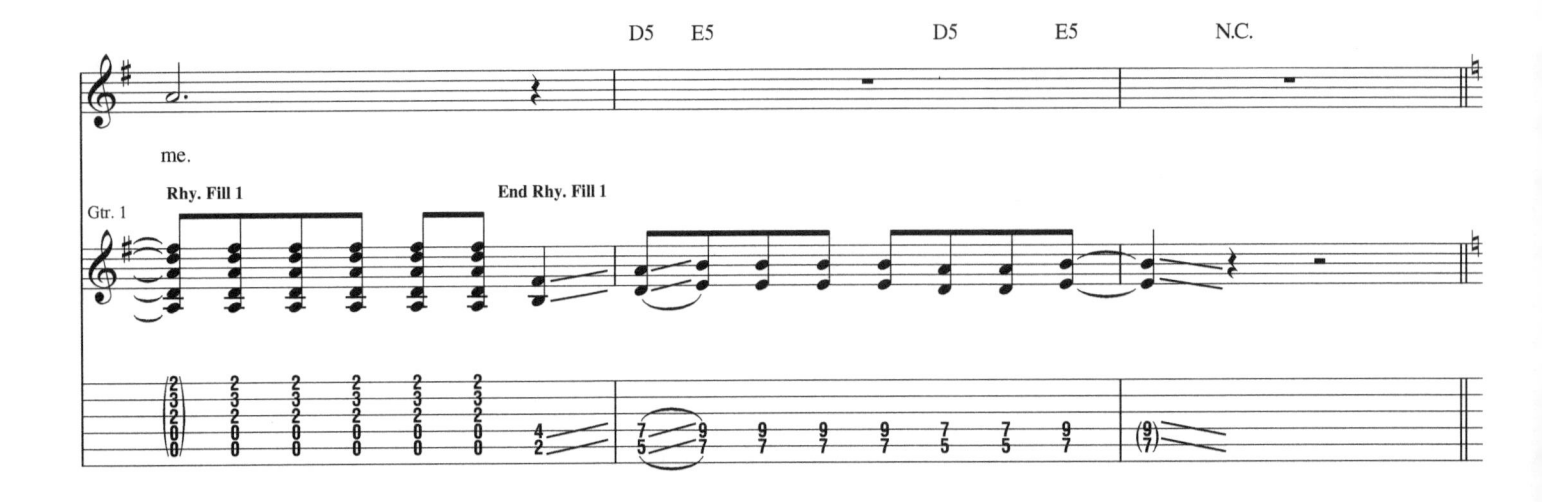

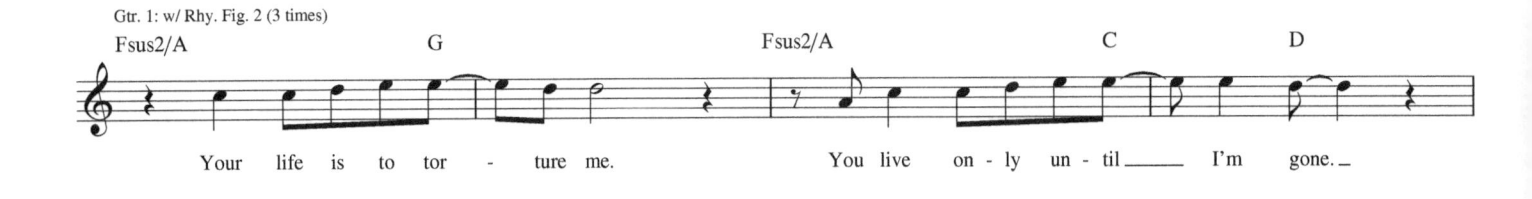

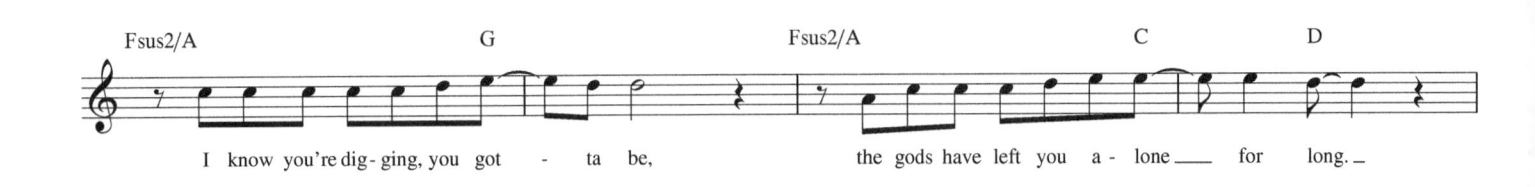

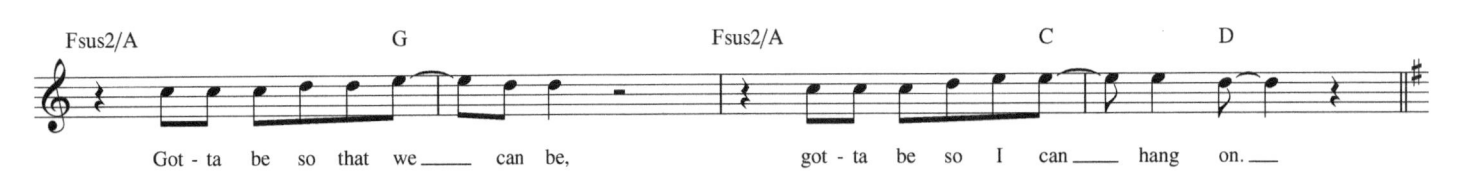

Interlude

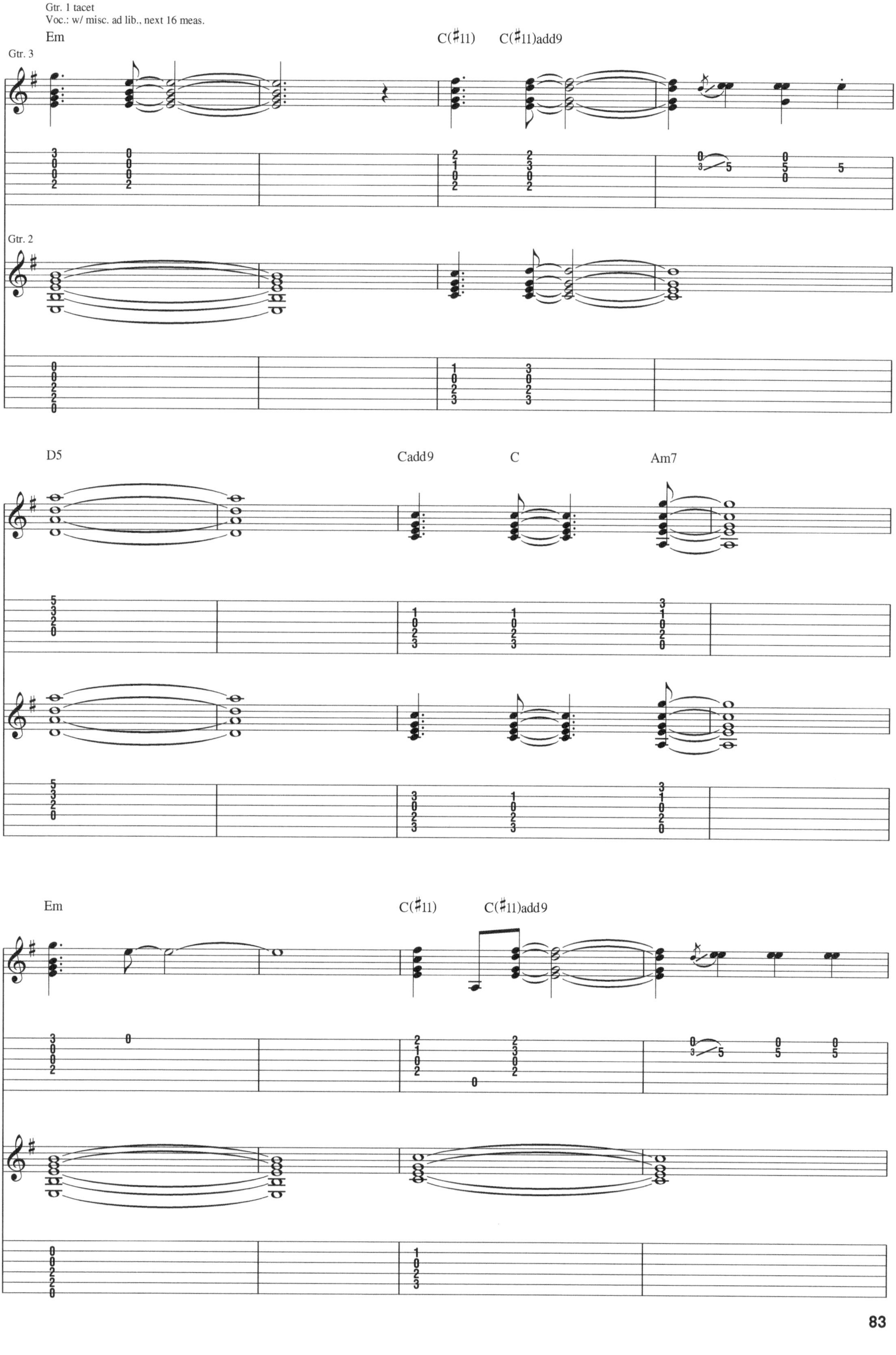
Gtr. 1 tacet
Voc.: w/ misc. ad lib., next 16 meas.
Em
C(♯11)
C(♯11)add9
Gtr. 3
Gtr. 2
D5
Cadd9
C
Am7
Em
C(♯11)
C(♯11)add9

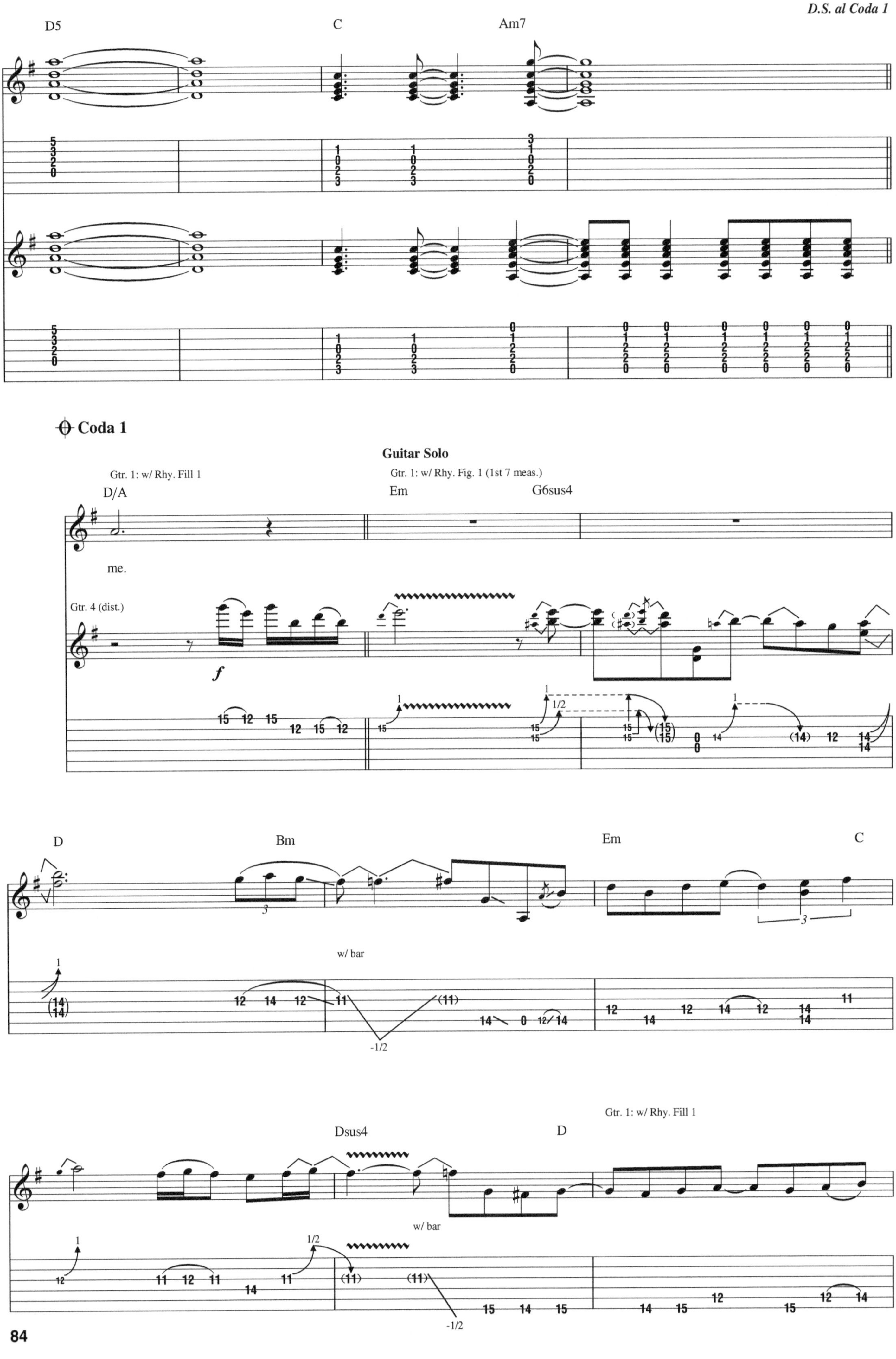
D.S. al Coda 1
D5
C
Am7
Coda 1
Guitar Solo
Gtr. 1: w/ Rhy. Fill 1
Gtr. 1: w/ Rhy. Fig. 1 (1st 7 meas.)
D/A
Em
G6sus4
me.
Gtr. 4 (dist.)
D
Bm
Em
C
w/ bar
Dsus4
D
Gtr. 1: w/ Rhy. Fill 1
w/ bar

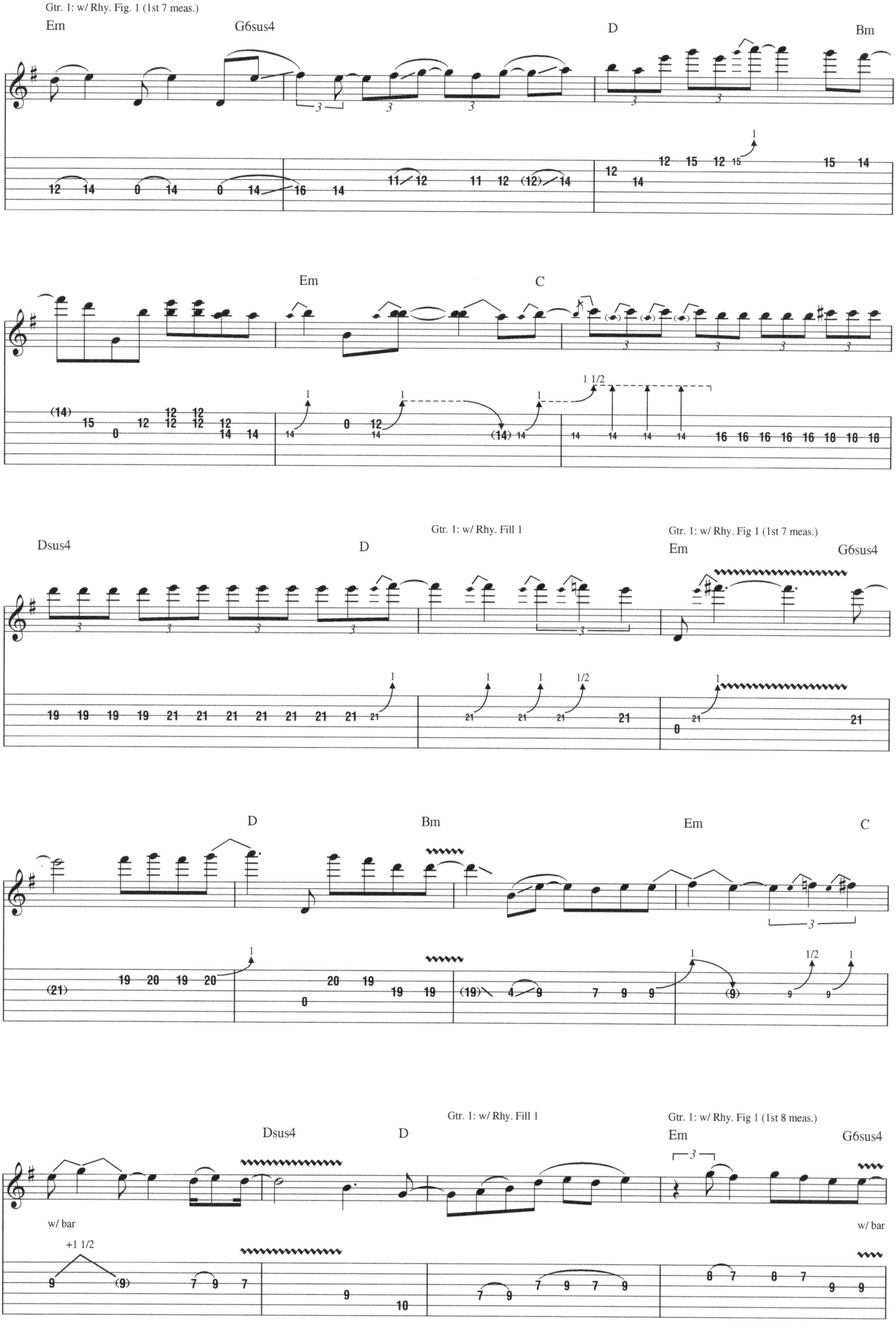
Gtr. 1: w/ Rhy. Fig. 1 (1st 7 meas.)
Em
G6sus4
D
Bm
Em
C
Dsus4
Gtr. 1: w/ Rhy. Fill 1
D
Gtr. 1: w/ Rhy. Fig 1 (1st 7 meas.)
Em
G6sus4
D
Bm
Em
C
w/ bar
Dsus4
Gtr. 1: w/ Rhy. Fill 1
D
Gtr. 1: w/ Rhy. Fig 1 (1st 8 meas.)
Em
G6sus4
w/ bar

Coda 2

The nightmare, you're standing there.

Now you'll have to decide the fate of my sanity.

from *You're Living All Over Me*

Sludgefeast

Words and Music by J Mascis

Intro

Moderately slow ♩ = 80

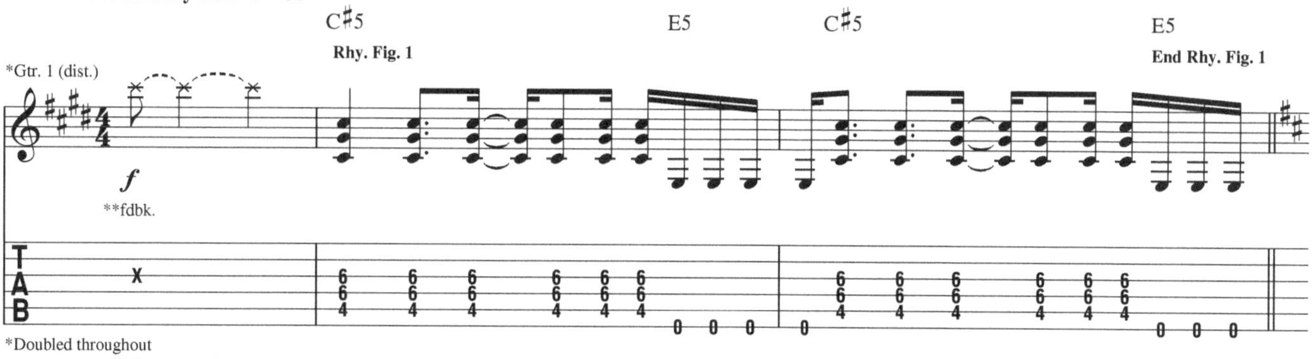

*Doubled throughout

**Microphonic fdbk., not caused by string vibration.

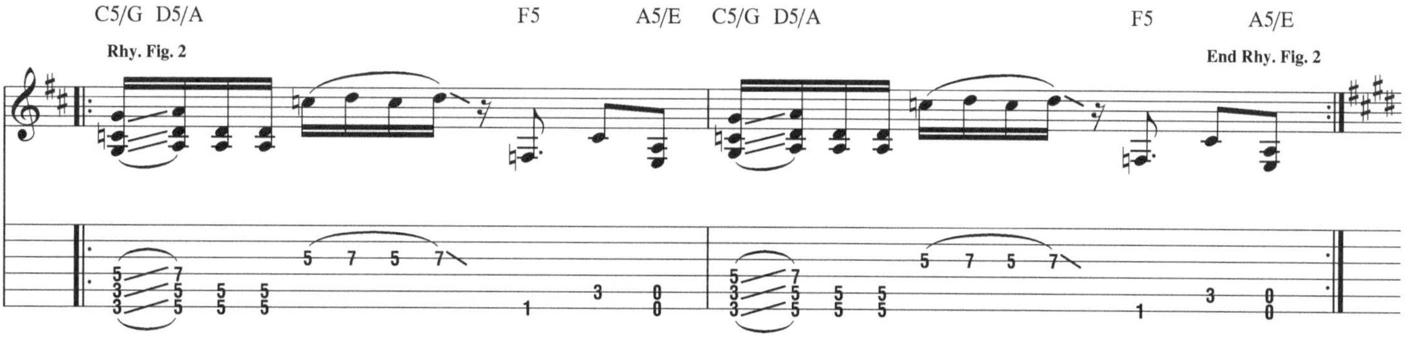

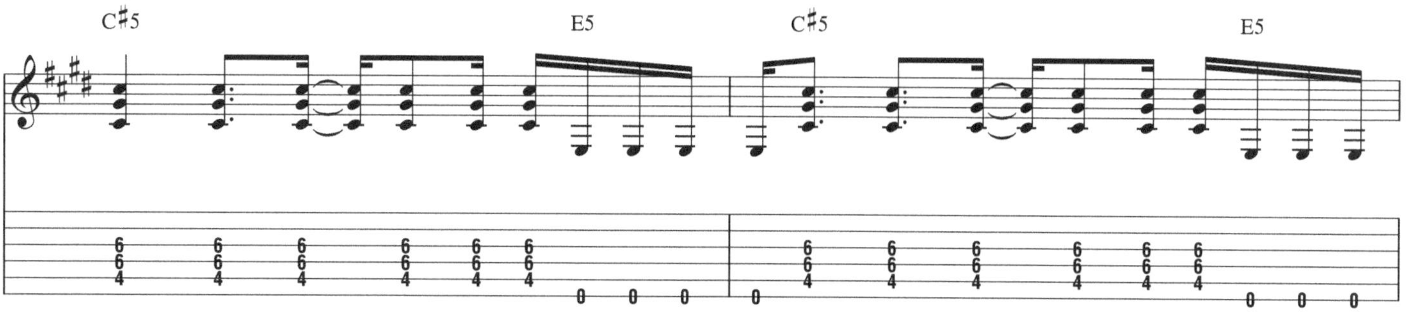

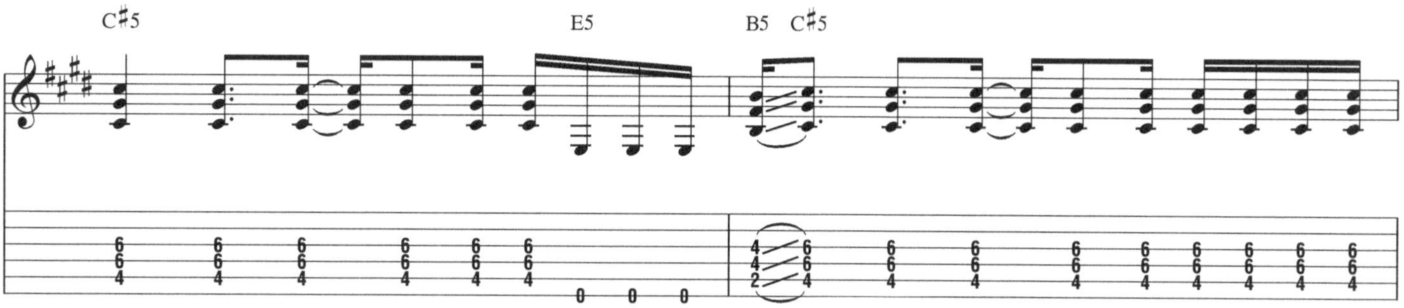

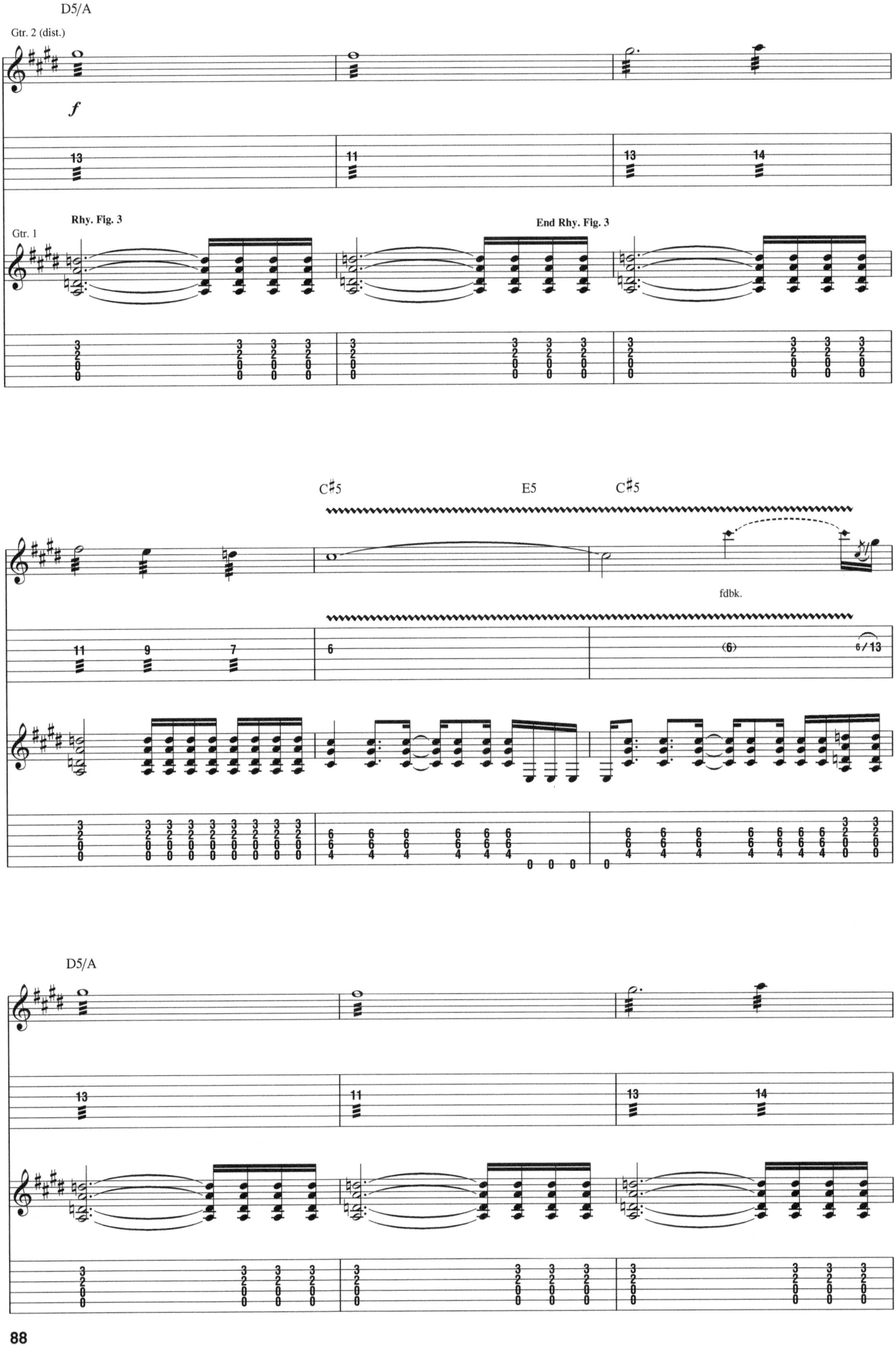
D5/A
Gtr. 2 (dist.)
f
Rhy. Fig. 3
End Rhy. Fig. 3
Gtr. 1
C♯5
E5
C♯5
fdbk.
D5/A

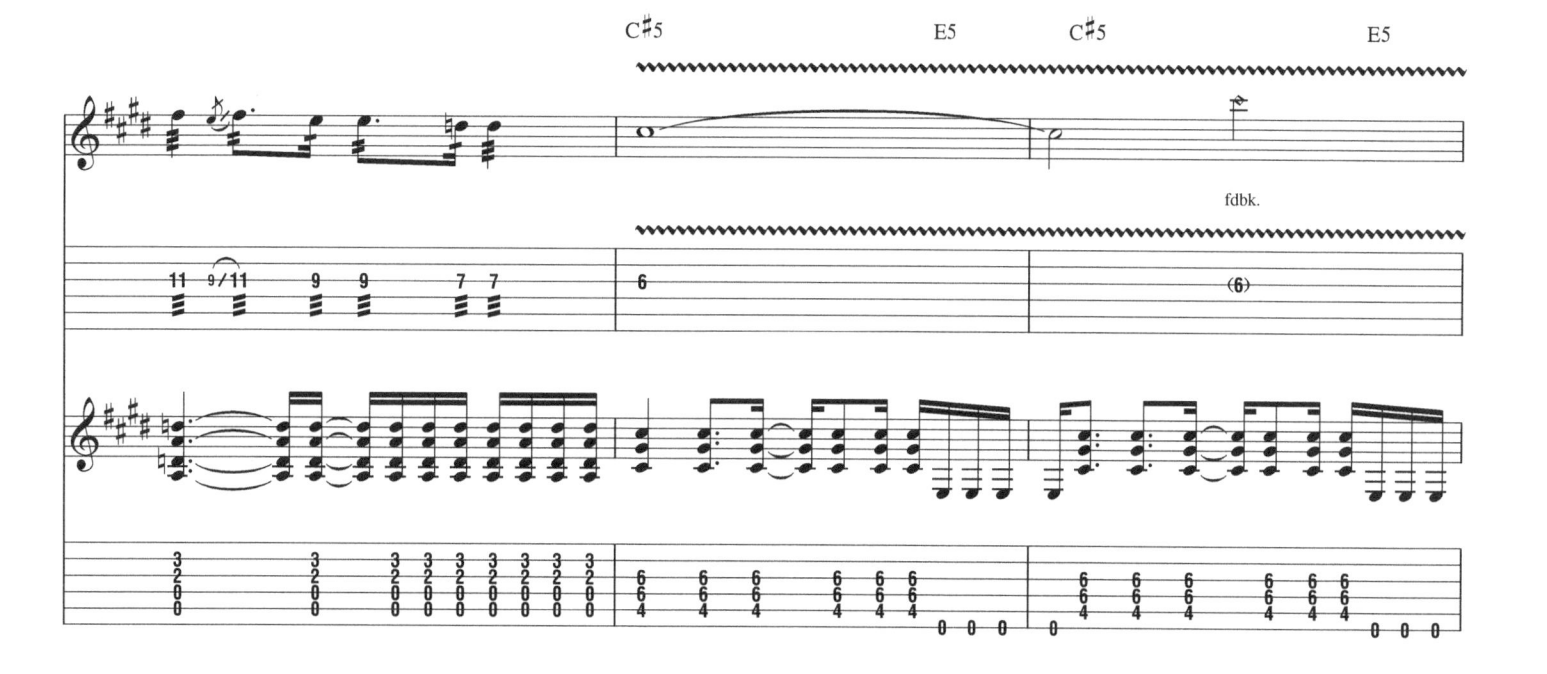

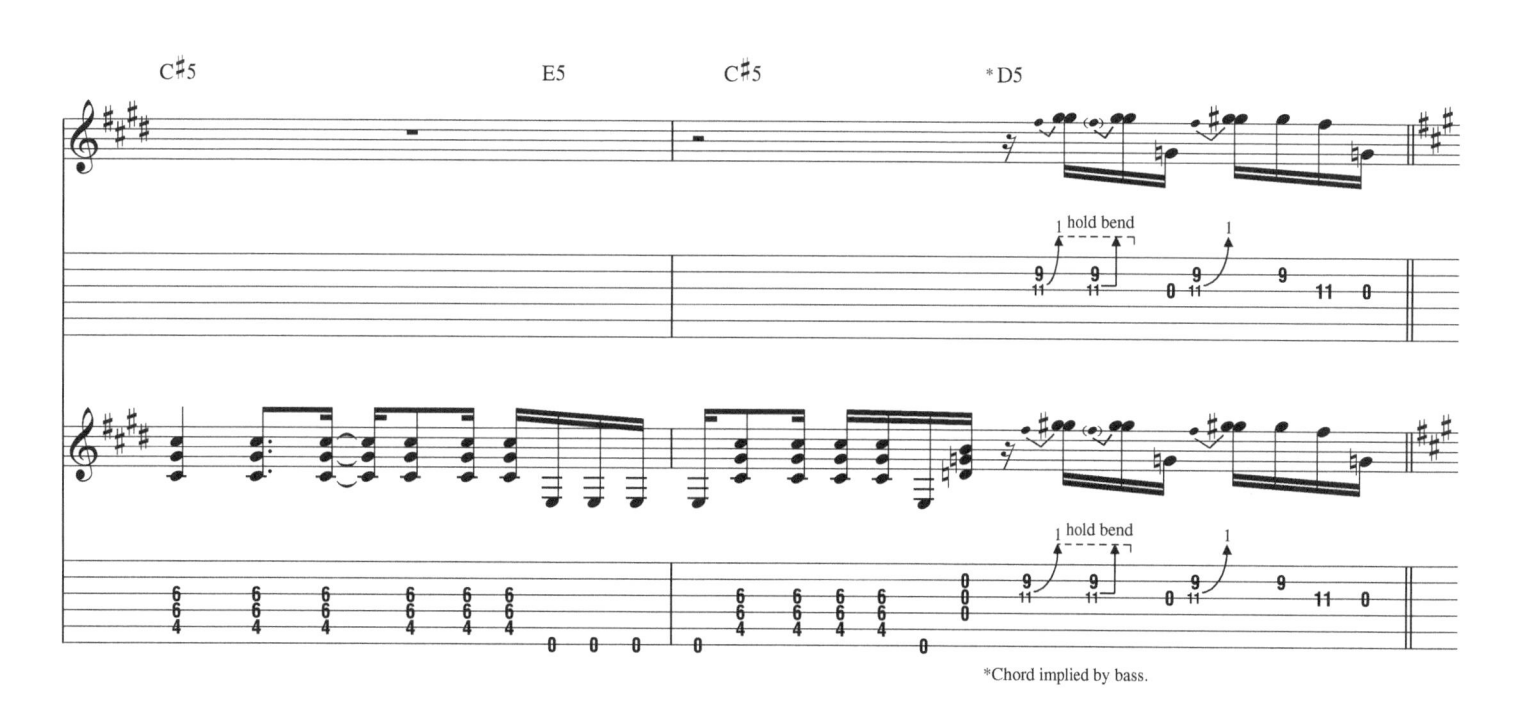

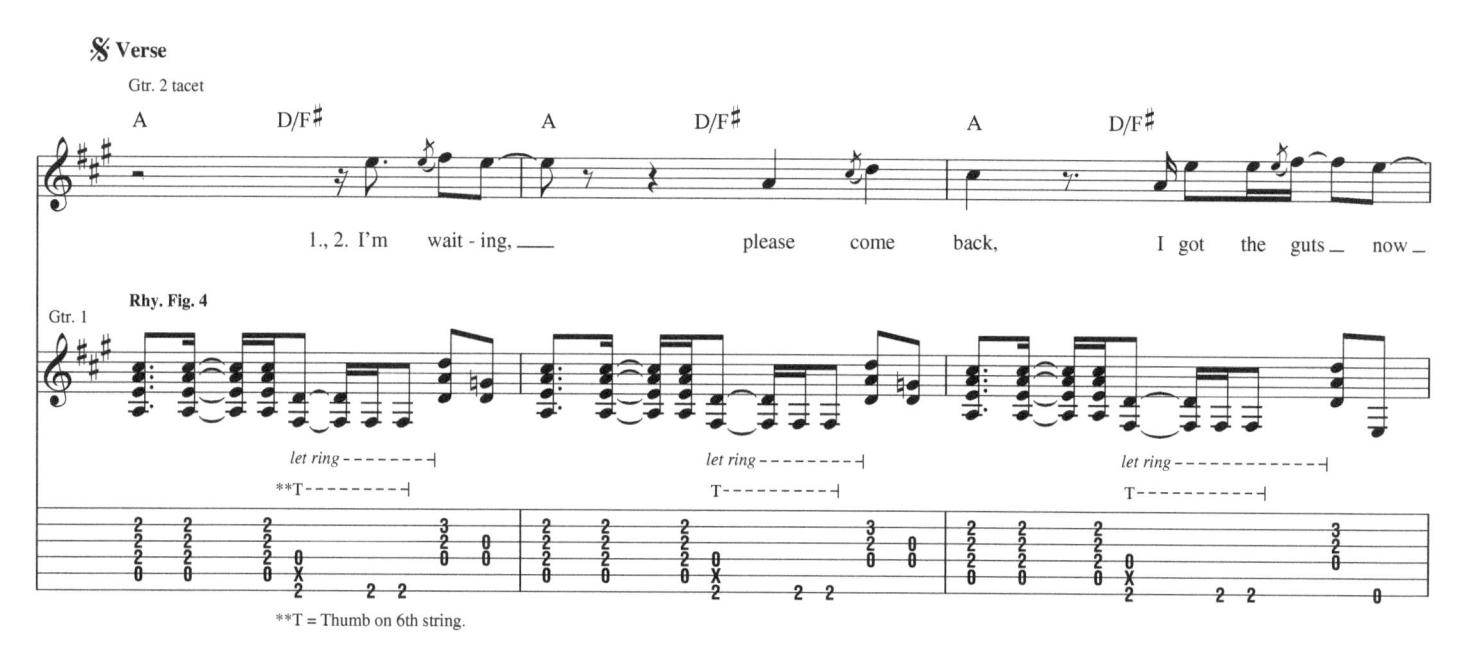

Verse

1., 2. I'm waiting, please come back, I got the guts now

Gtr. 1: w/ Rhy. Fig. 4 (1 3/4 times)
Gtr. 2 tacet
B5
A
D/F♯
A
D/F♯
to meet your eye. Those guts are kill - ing, but I can't stop
Gtr. 2
Riff A
End Riff A
Gtr. 1
End Rhy. Fig. 4
Gtr. 2: w/ Riff A
A
D/F♯
B5
now, got - ta con - nect with you, girl, or I'll for - get how.
To Coda
A
D/F♯
A
D/F♯
A
D/F♯
Please, wan - na hang a - round. Can drop you un - der
Gtr. 2: w/ Riff A (1st meas.)
B5
E5
what it is we found.
Gtr. 1
P.S.
Harm.

Interlude

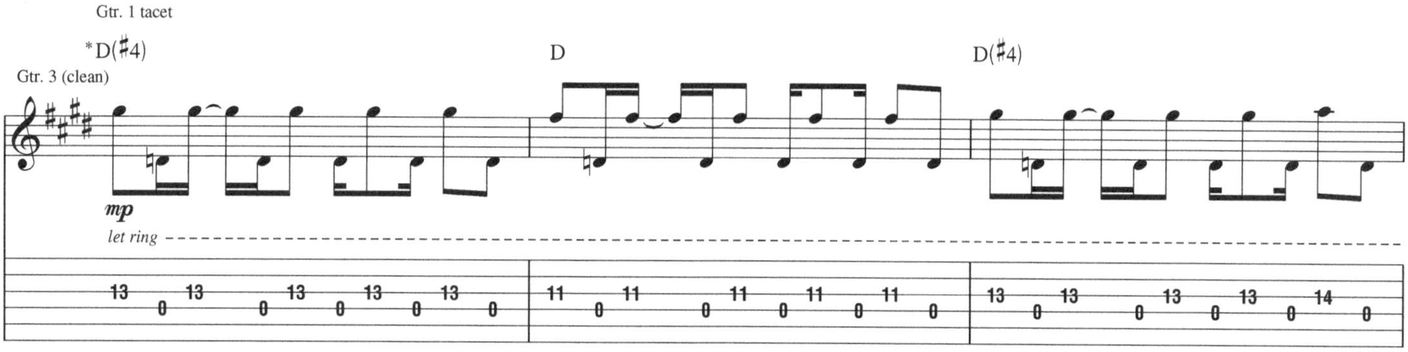

*Chord symbols reflect overall harmony.

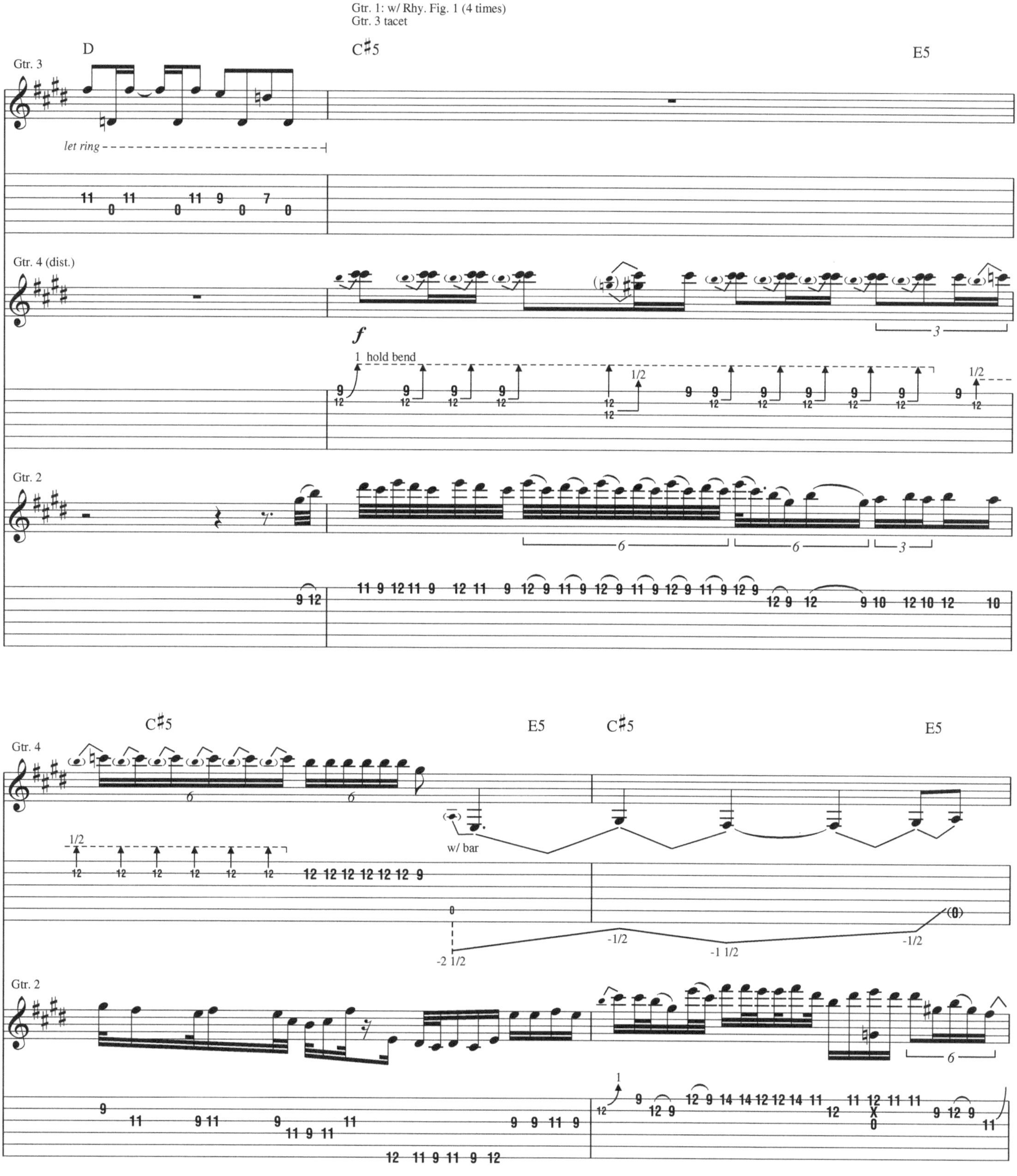

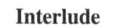

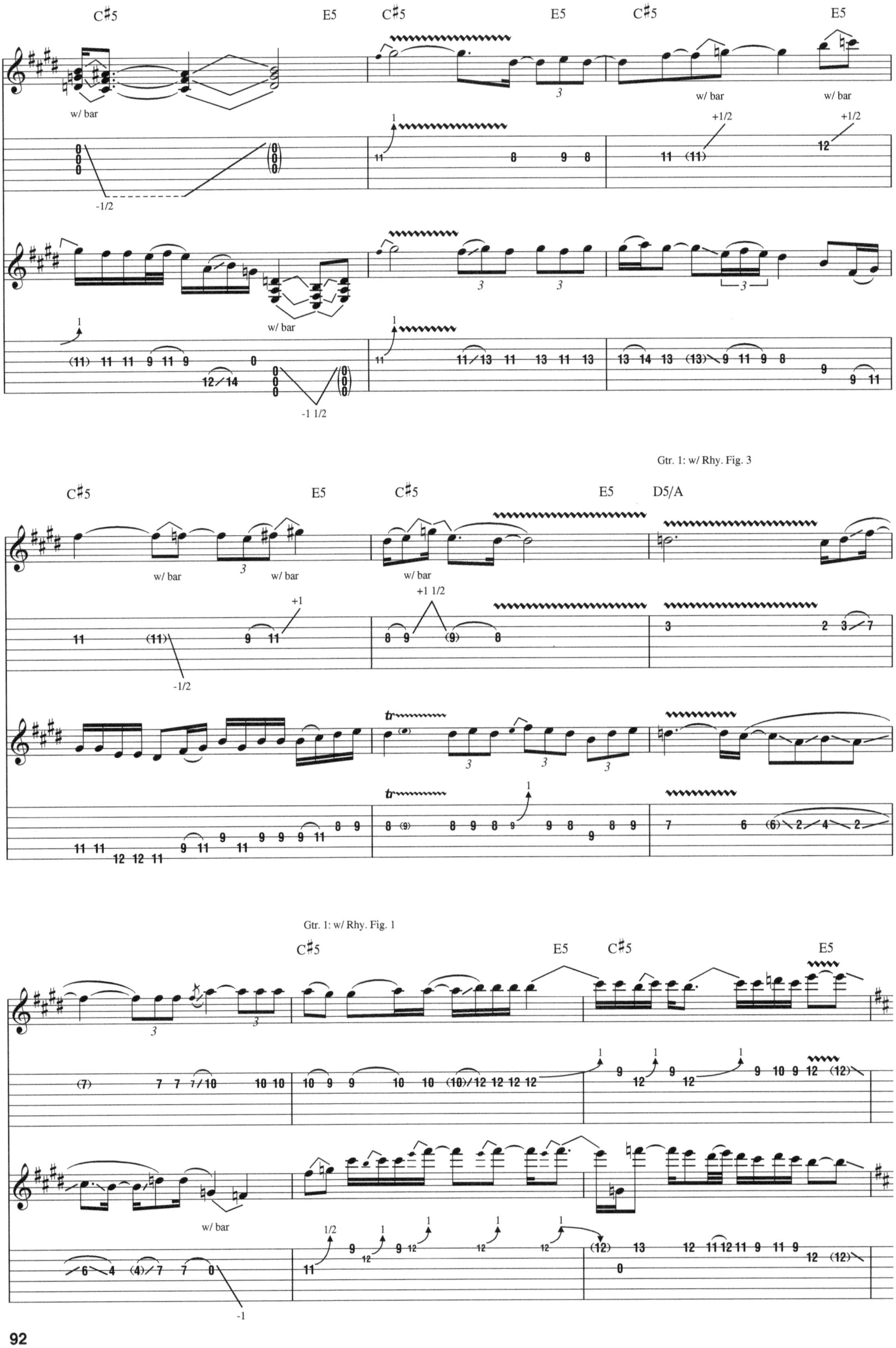
C♯5
E5
w/ bar
Gtr. 1: w/ Rhy. Fig. 3
D5/A
Gtr. 1: w/ Rhy. Fig. 1

what it is we found.

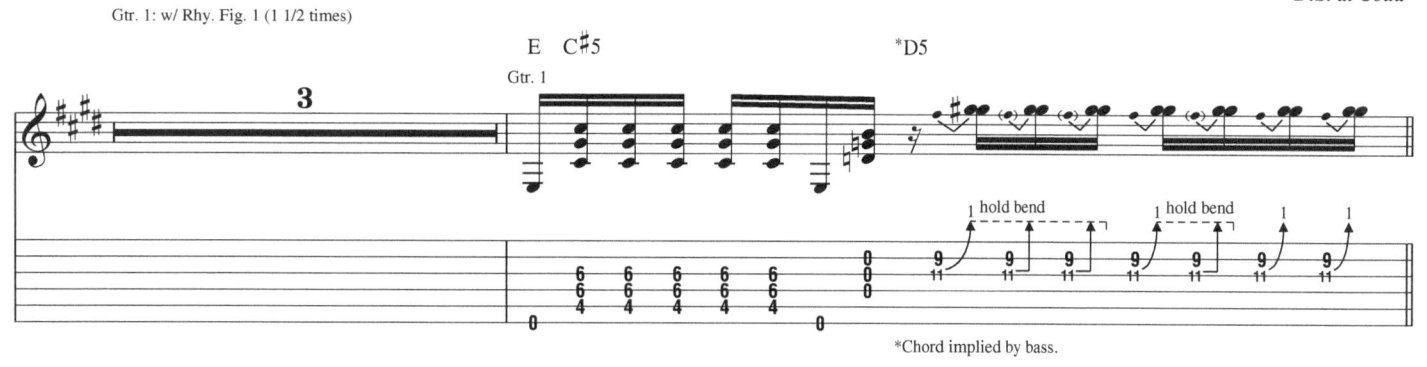

Free time
G5
Gtr. 4
Gtr. 4
Gtr. 1
divisi
Gtr. 5
w/ bar
8va
loco
Harm.
slack
*Indiscernable noise w/ bar.
Outro
Fast ♩ = 175
Gtrs. 4 & 5 tacet
F♯5
G5
E5
G5
Rhy. Fig. 5
End Rhy. Fig. 5
Gtr. 1
P.M.
P.M.
Guitar Solo
Gtr. 1: w/ Rhy. Fig. 5 (till fade)
F♯5
G5
E5
Gtr. 2
G5
F♯5
G5

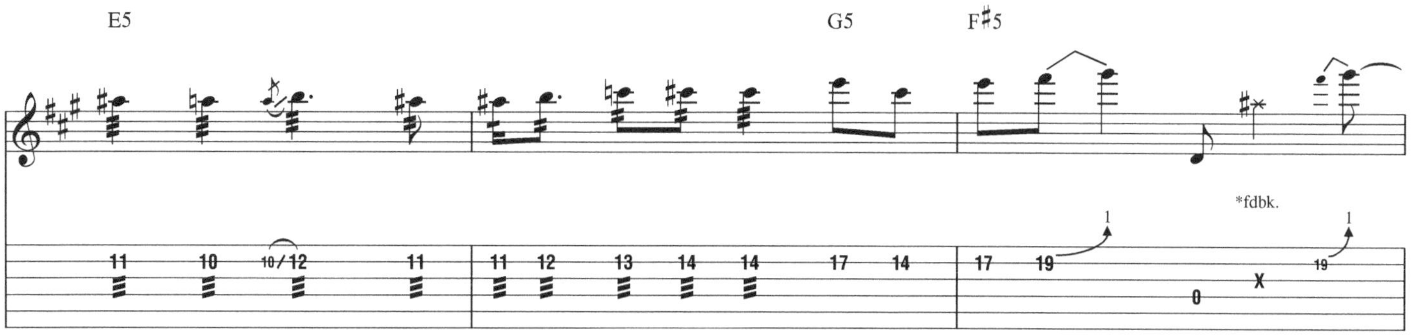

*Microphonic fdbk., not caused by string vibration.

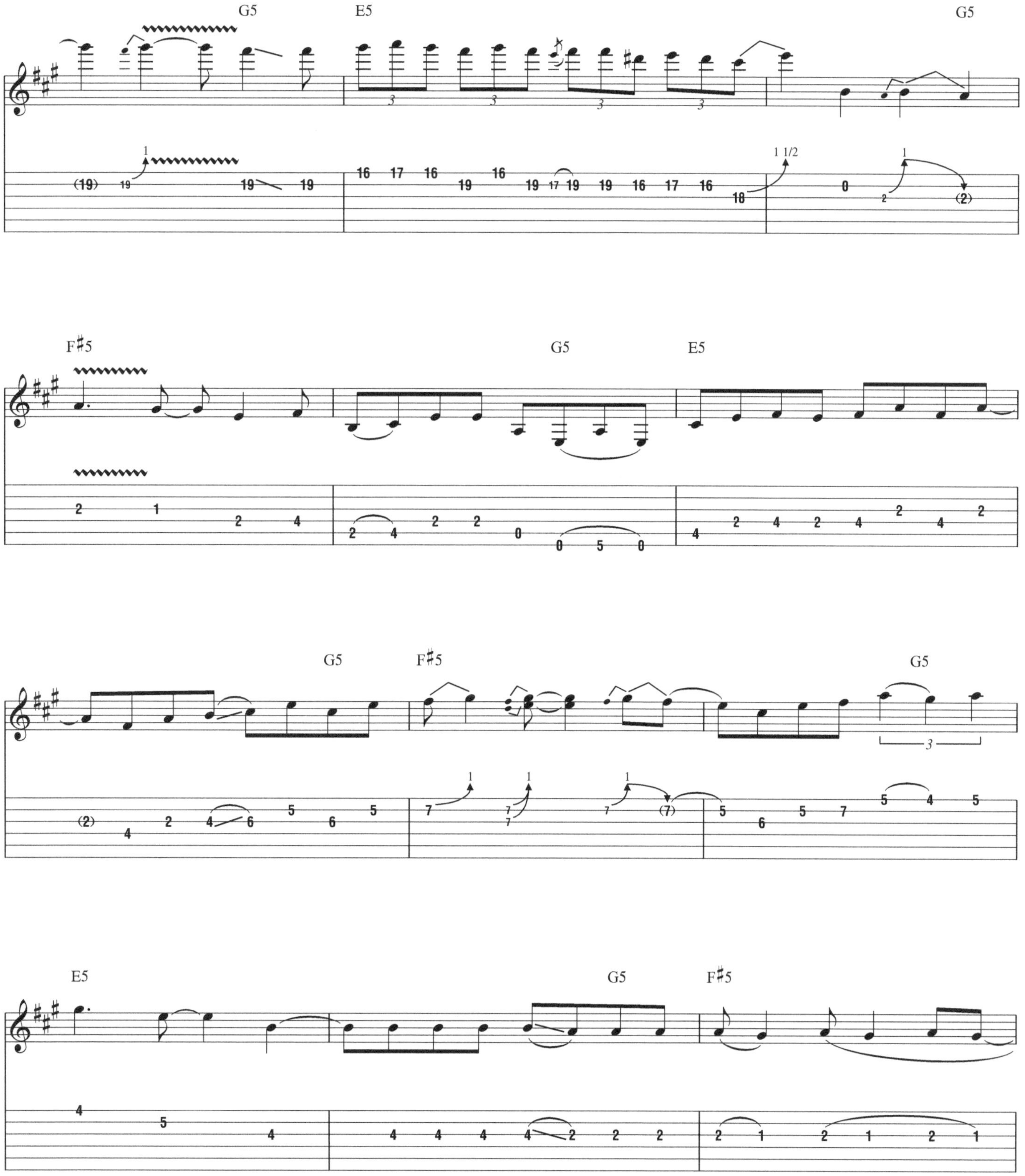

G5
E5
G5
F♯5
G5
E5
G5
F♯5
G5
E5
Begin fade
G5
F♯5
Harm.
w/ bar
-1/2
Fade out
G5
E5
G5

from *Where You Been*

Start Choppin

Words and Music by J Mascis

98

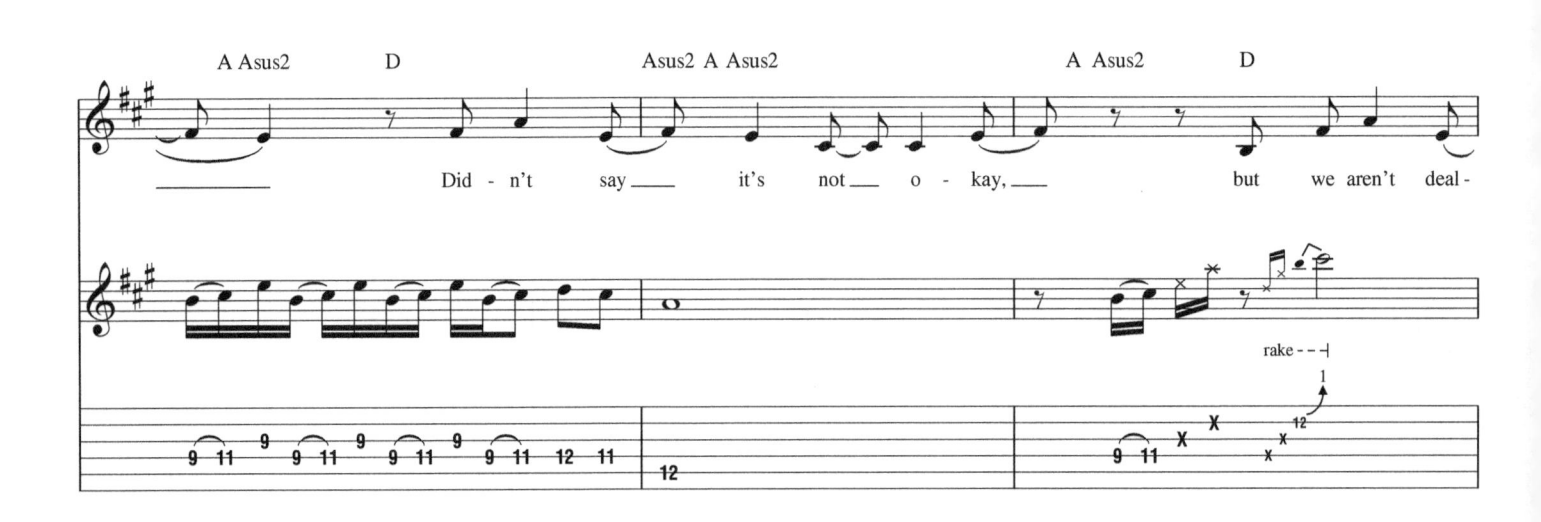

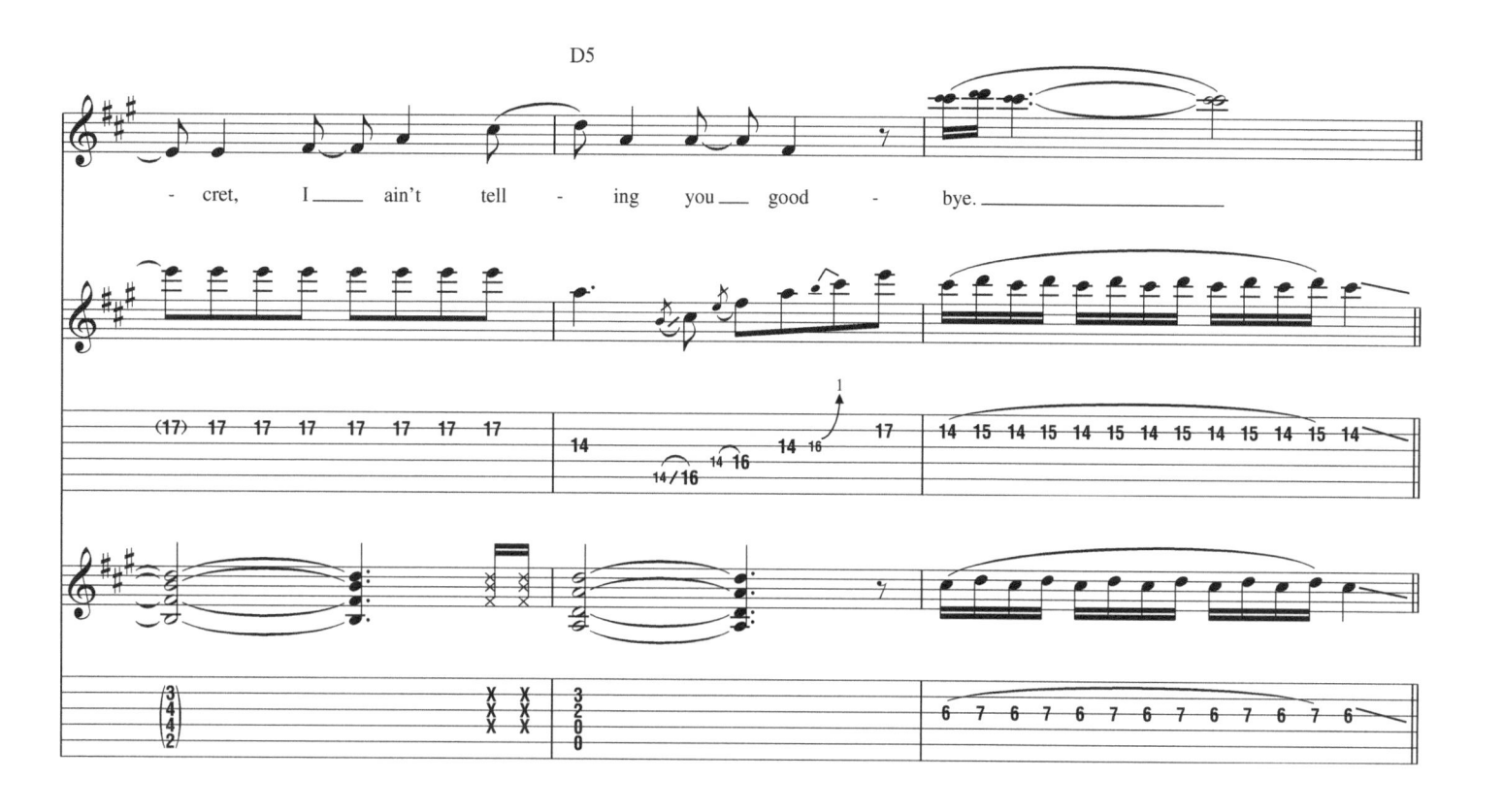

-cret, I ain't telling you goodbye.

Interlude
Gtr. 2 tacet

2. A, it's the last
3. Oh, when you call

Rhy. Fig. 2
Gtrs. 3 & 4
End Rhy. Fig. 2

**w/ pick & fingers   P.M.   P.M.   *let ring*   P.M.   P.M.   *let ring*

**Fingers on high E string only.

Verse
Gtrs. 3 & 4: w/ Rhy. Fig. 2 (2 times)

— thing on my mind, still you won't let things unwind, spinning tight-
— it's just not fair, uh, it's the last thing you should share, I can't deal,

-er 'round your head, a, can't you hear a word I said? A, I ain't tell-
I'll let you know, still I wish you'd let it go.

99

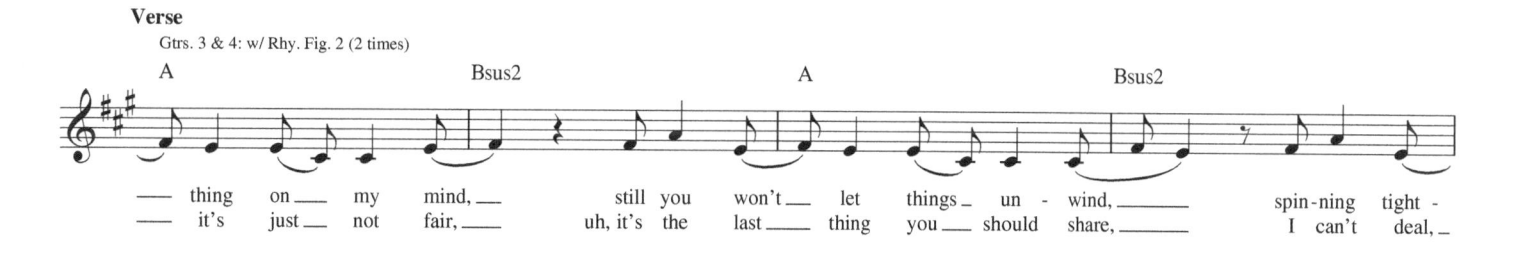

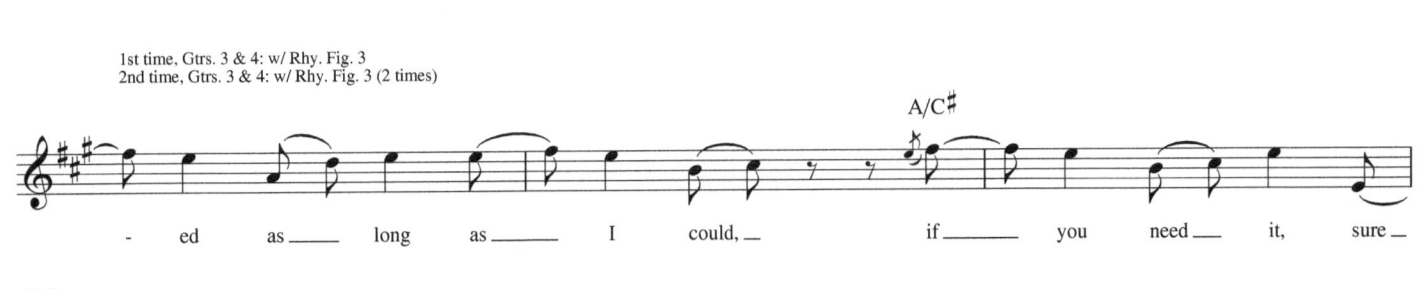

Chorus

-ing you a secret, I ain't telling you goodbye.

1.

2.

Bridge

D5   A/C#

bye. I'm telling you for one last time, it's not

E7   D5

just you, the problem's mine to hide. I wait-

1st time, Gtrs. 3 & 4: w/ Rhy. Fig. 3
2nd time, Gtrs. 3 & 4: w/ Rhy. Fig. 3 (2 times)

A/C#

-ed as long as I could, if you need it, sure

101

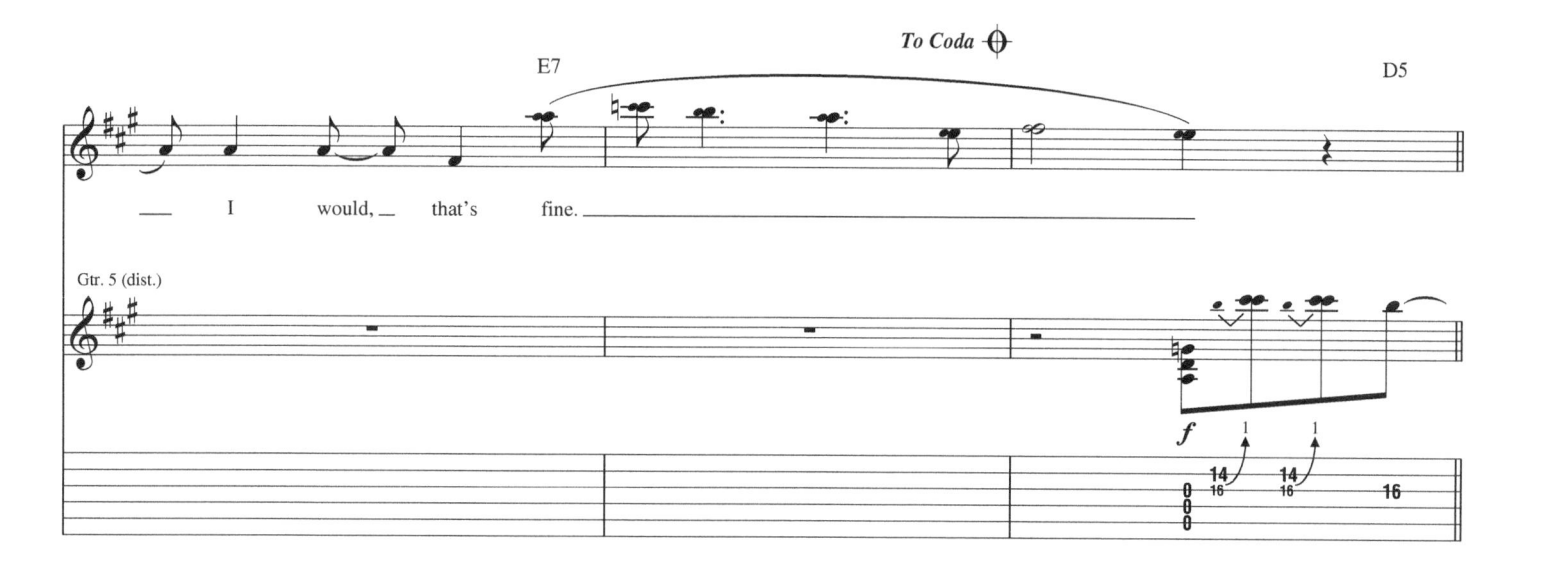

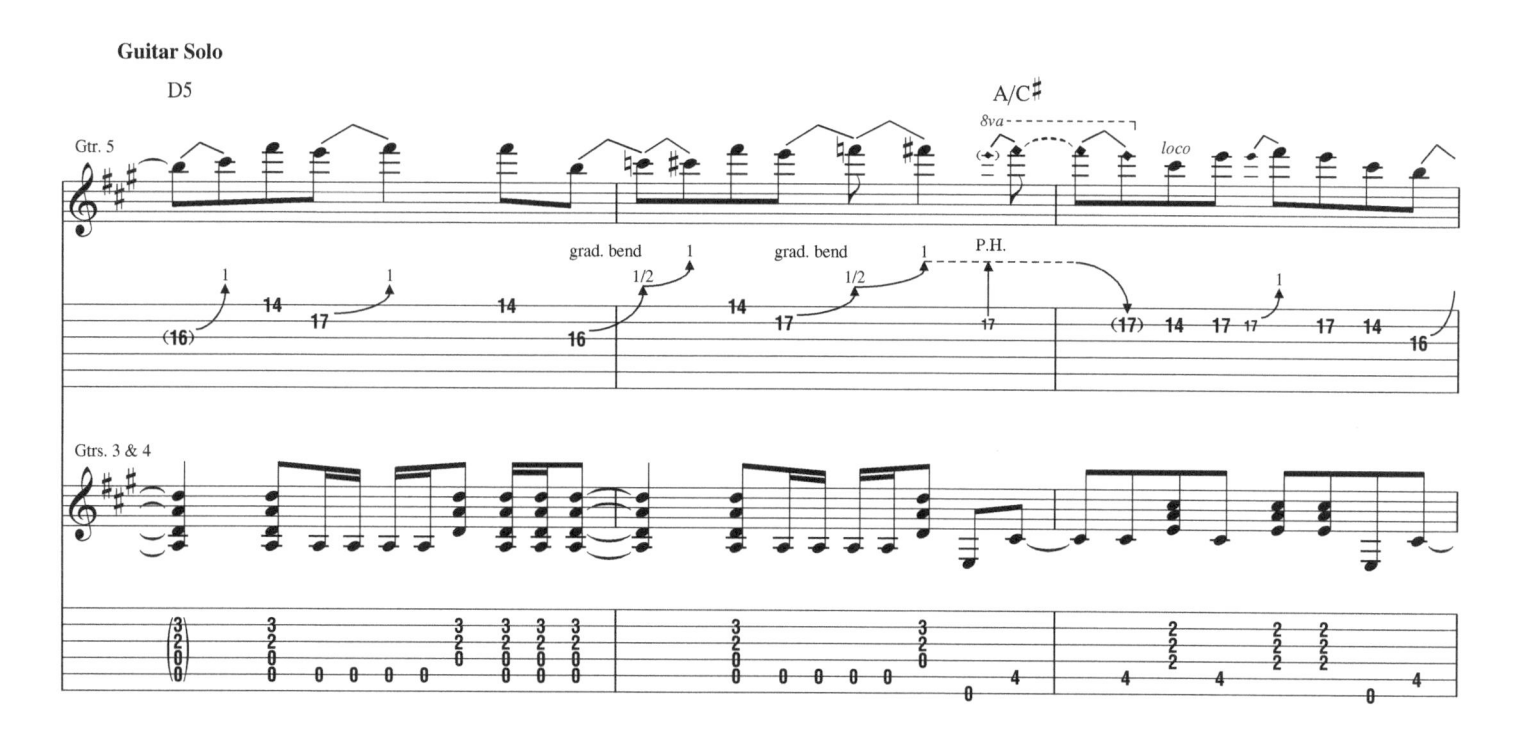

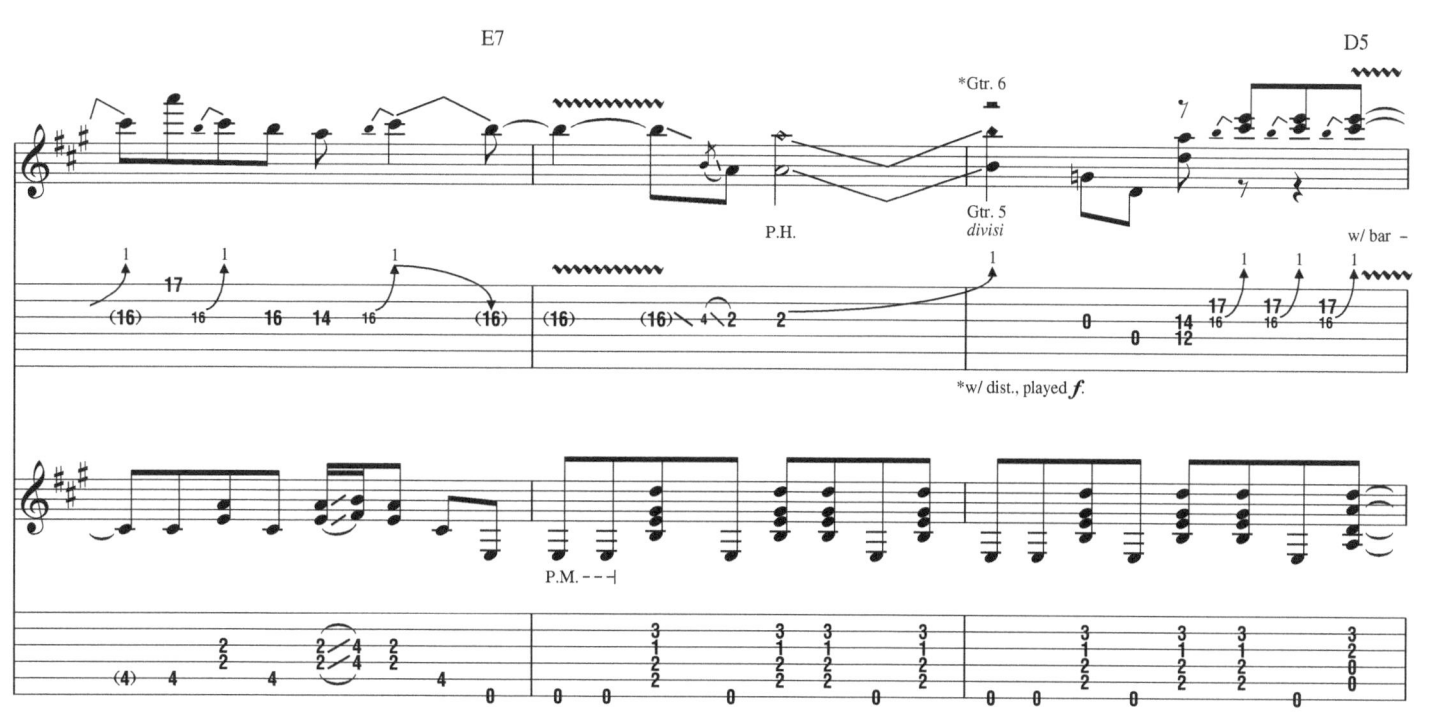

Gtrs. 3 & 4: w/ Rhy. Fig. 3 (1st 3 meas.)
Gtr. 5 tacet
A/C♯
Gtr. 6
8va
loco
w/ bar
grad. bend
E7
Gtrs. 3 & 4
P.M.
Asus2 A Asus2
A Asus2
D
Rhy. Fig. 4
End Rhy. Fig. 4
Gtrs. 3 & 4: w/ Rhy. Fig. 4 (3 times)

Asus2 A Asus2
A Asus2
D
hold bend
Asus2 A Asus2
A Asus2
D
4. Well, there's no go -
8va
w/ bar
Verse
Gtrs. 3 & 4: w/ Rhy. Fig. 4 (3 1/2 times)
Gtr. 6 tacet
Asus2 A Asus2
A Asus2
D
Asus2 A Asus2
- in' back to that, I'm so numb can't e - ven re - act.
8va
loco
*Open strings ring sympathetically.
A Asus2
D
Asus2 A Asus2
A Asus2
D
Asus2 A Asus2
Did - n't say it's not o - kay, but we aren't deal - ing the same way.
Chorus
A Asus2
D
Bm
I ain't tell - ing you a se - cret, I ain't tell -
Gtrs. 3 & 4

Interlude
Gtrs. 3 & 4: w/ Rhy. Fig. 2 (1 1/4 times)
D5
A
- ing you good - bye.
Bsus2
A
Bsus2
A
Good - bye.
Good - bye.
D.S. al Coda
Bsus2
A
Bsus2
D5
Good - bye.
I'm tell -
Gtrs. 3 & 4
let ring
P.M.
P.M.
let ring
Coda
D5
A/C♯
I've tak - en a - way a lot of stuff I'm tell -
E7
D5
- ing you it's rough, but not good - bye.
Gtr. 5
hold bend

Guitar Solo

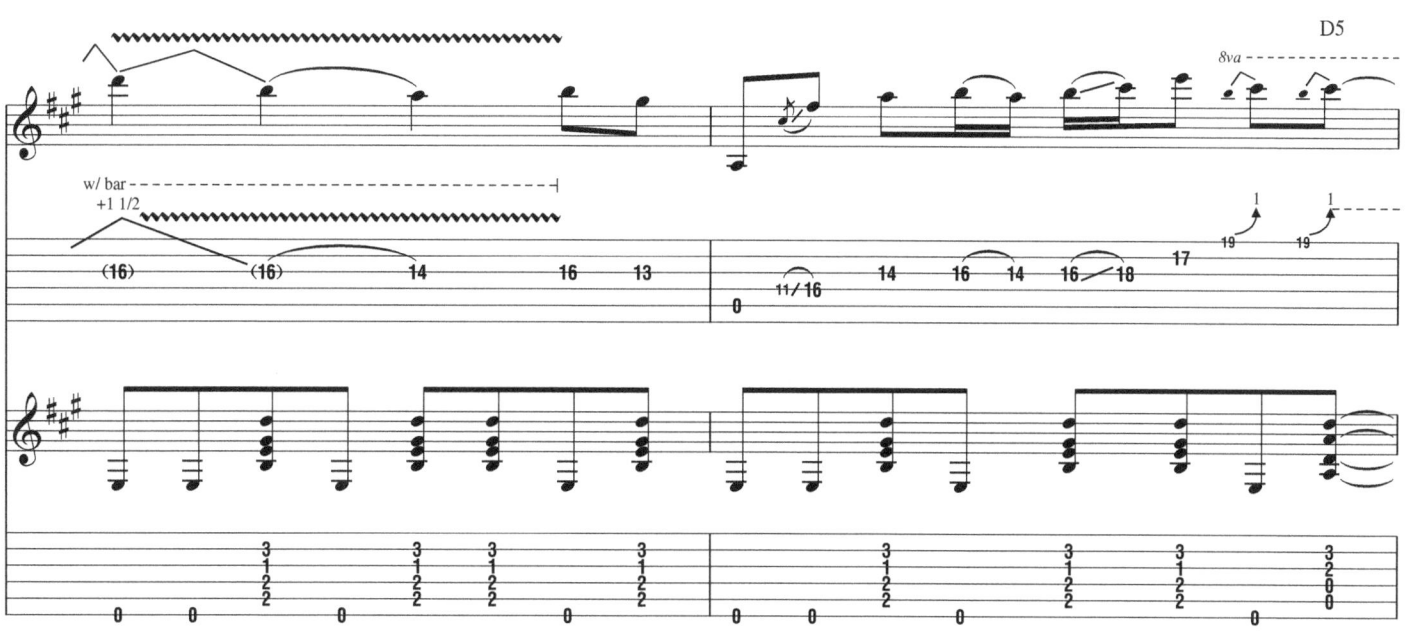

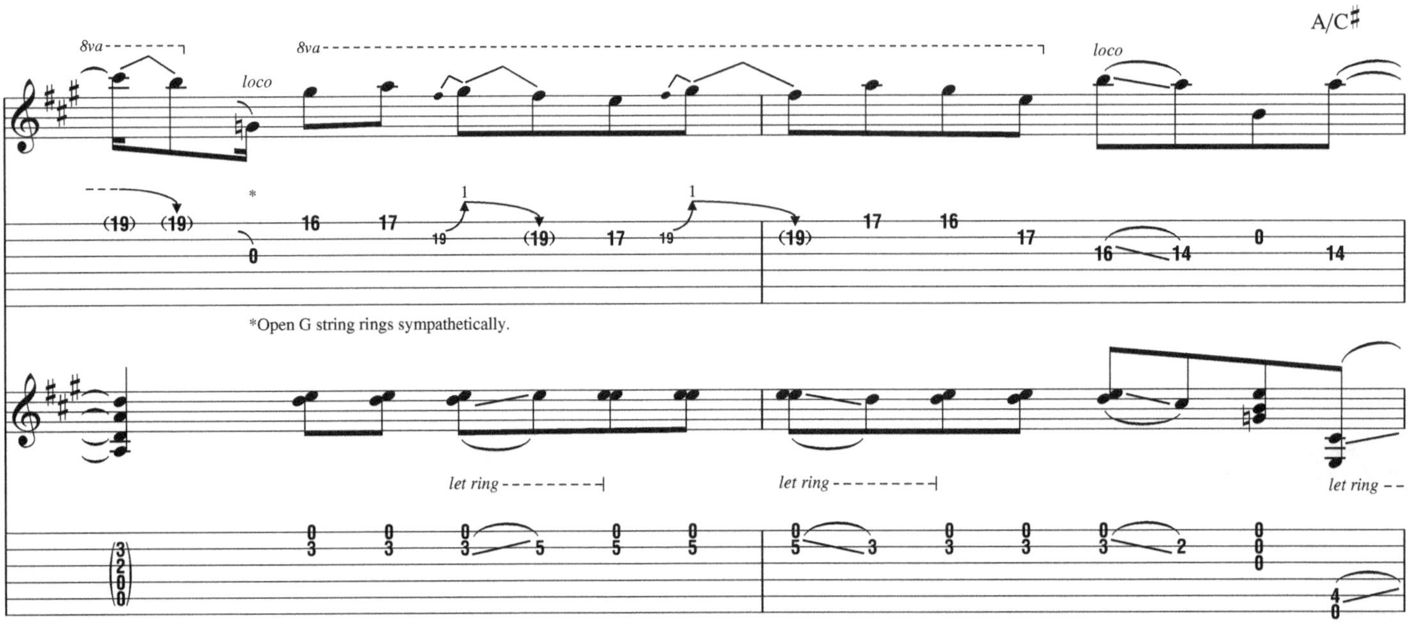
A/C♯
8va
loco
let ring
*Open G string rings sympathetically.

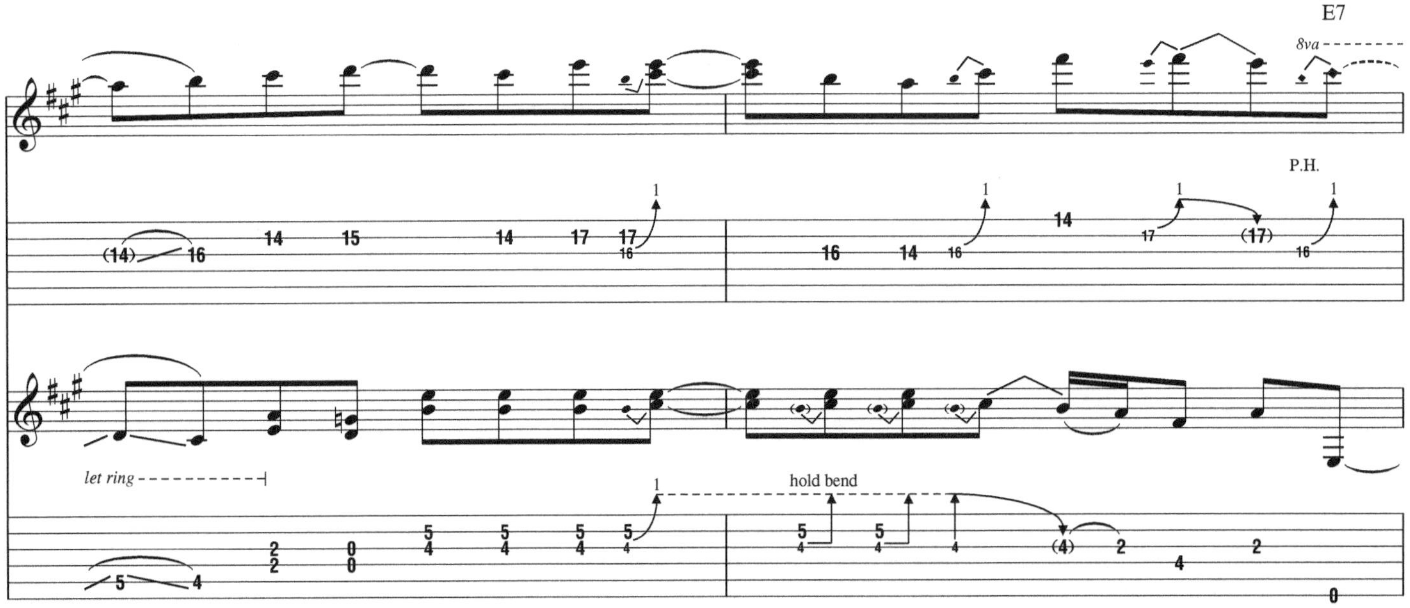
E7
8va
P.H.
let ring
hold bend

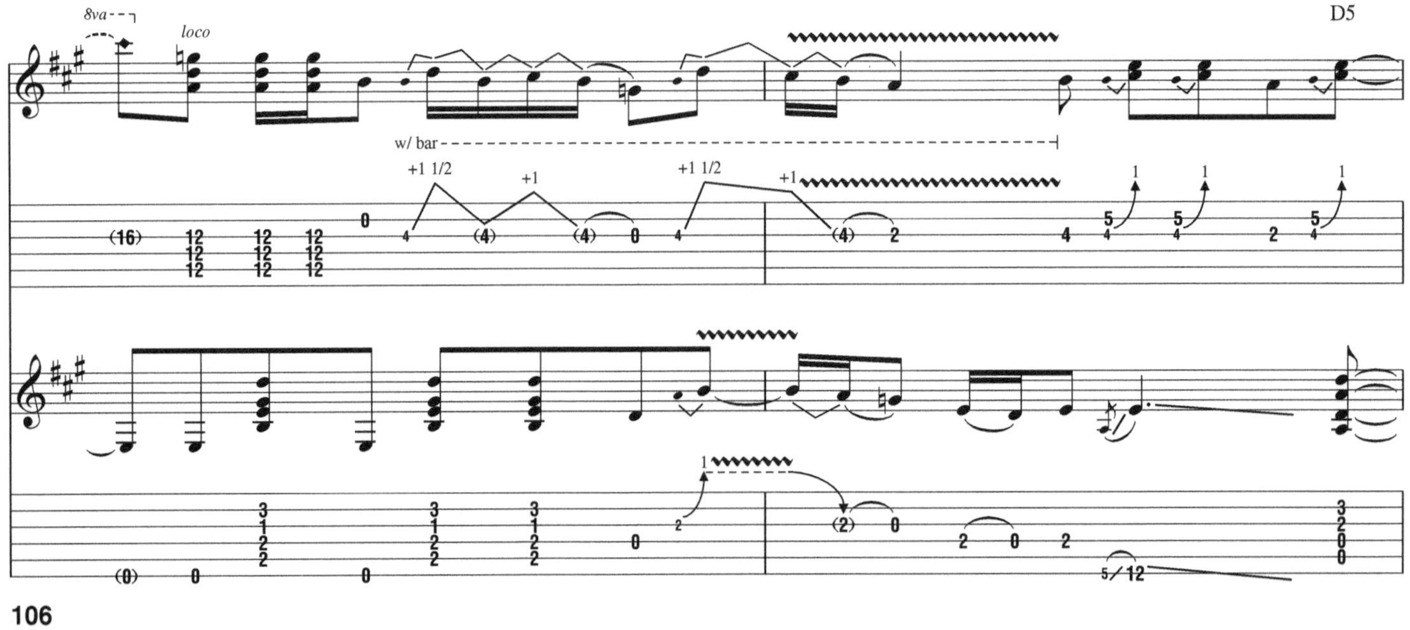
D5
8va
loco
w/ bar
+1 1/2
+1

107

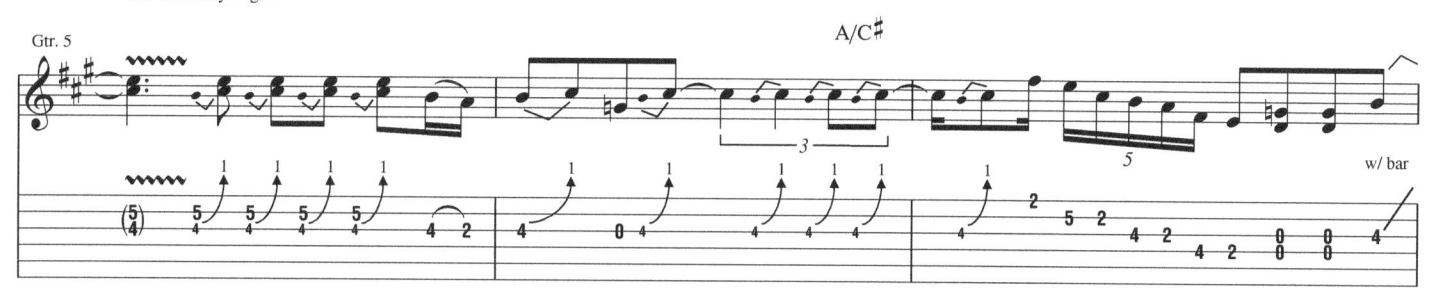

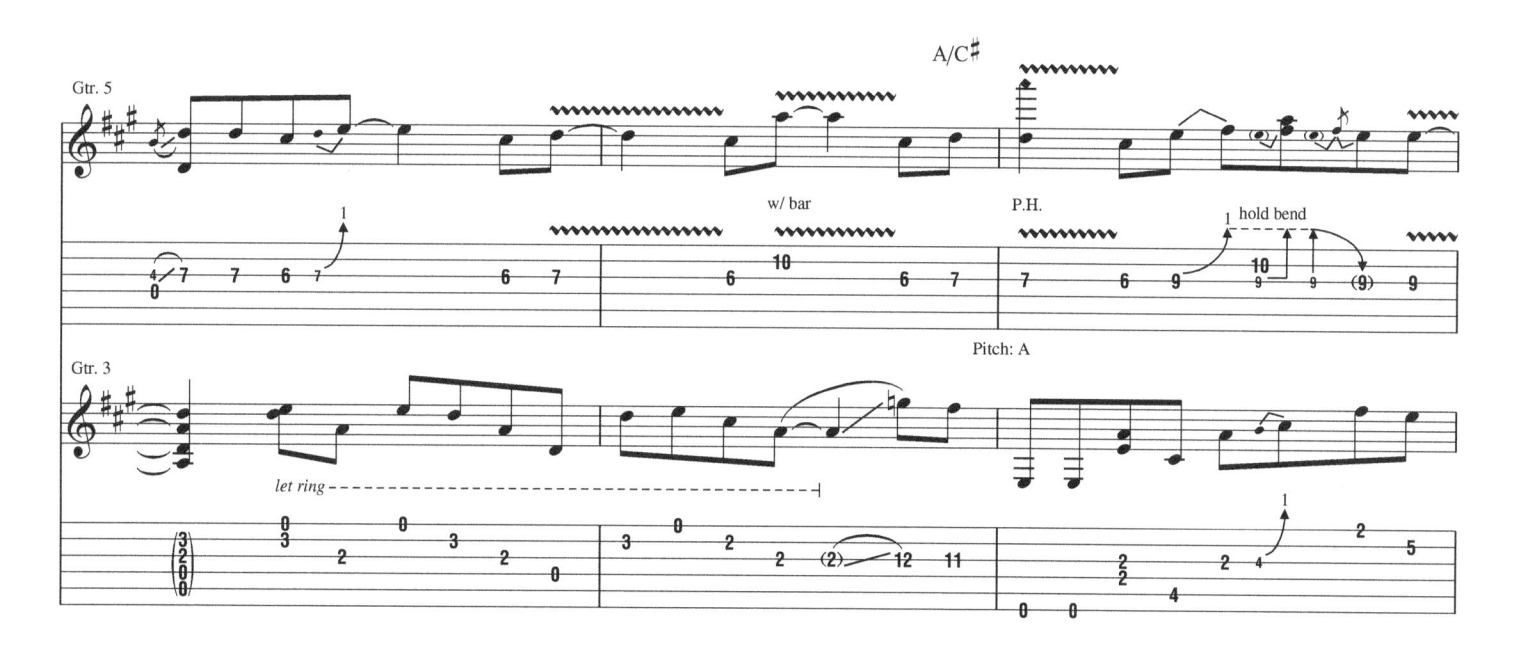

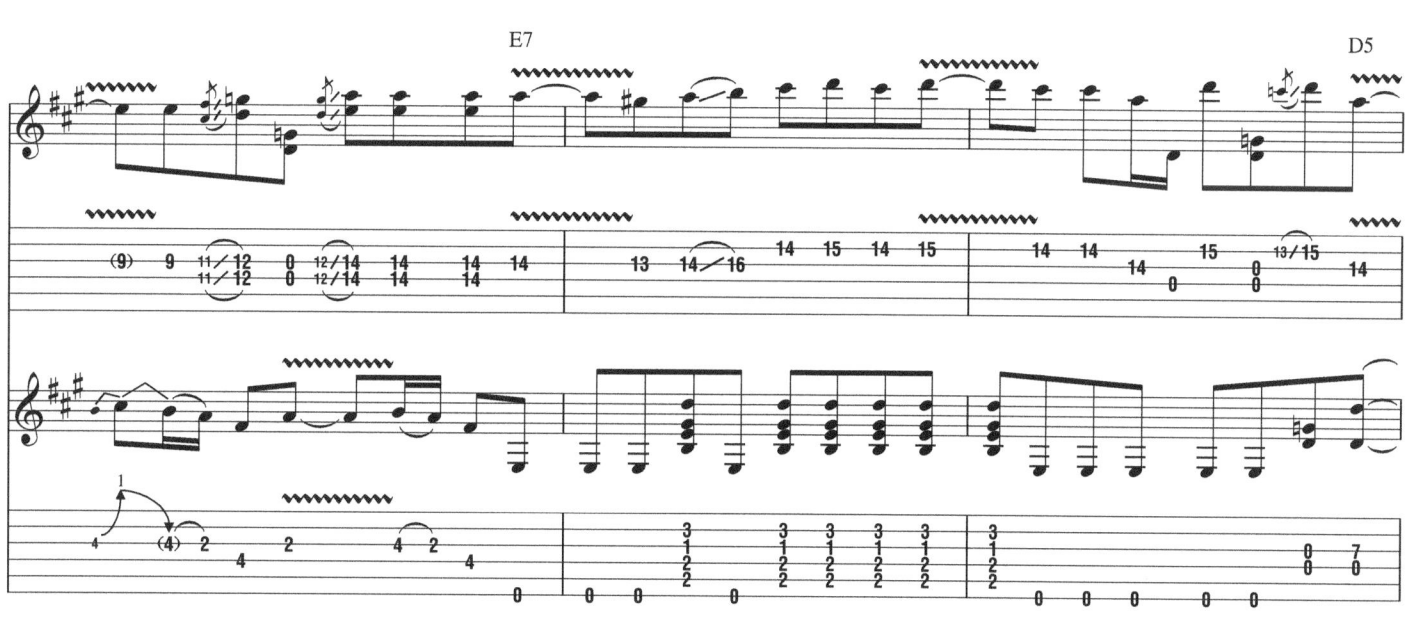

Begin fade
A/C♯
8va
loco
grad. bend
E7
D5
8va
loco
P.H.
Harm.
Fade out
A/C♯
w/ bar

from *Green Mind*

Thumb

Words and Music by J Mascis

Intro
Moderately slow ♩ = 71

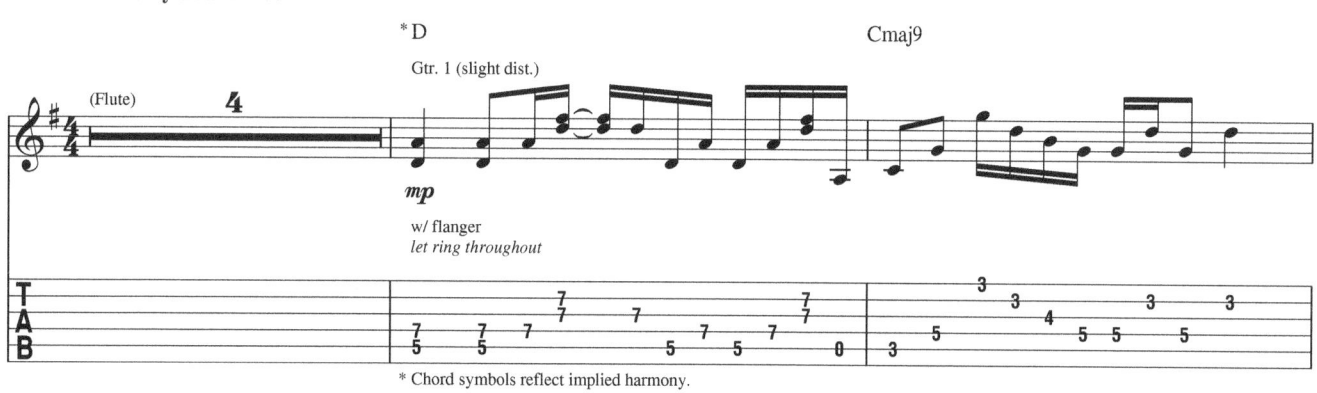

* Chord symbols reflect implied harmony.

Chorus

There nev-er real-ly is a good

Riff A

Copyright © 1991 Spam As The Bread Music
All Rights Administered by Chrysalis Songs
All Rights Reserved   Used by Permission

Gadd4/B G/B A7sus4 Cmaj9
time. There's al - ways noth - ing much to say.
Gadd4/B G/B A7sus4 Cmaj9
A, pret - ty good, not do - ing that
Gadd4/B G/B A7sus4 Cmaj9 N.C.
fine, get - ting up most ev - 'ry day.
Verse
D Cmaj9 D
1. Step - pin' out, I tried to fix it.
2. An ex - cuse is all you're in for,
3. There's a time, just let me know now,

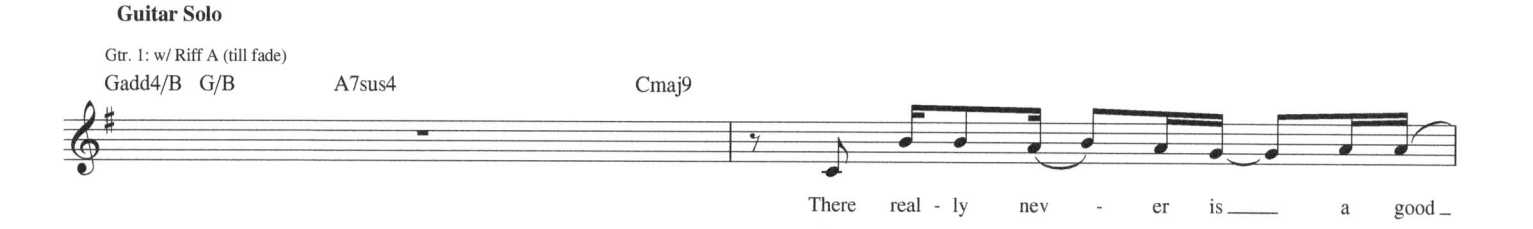

Cmaj9   D

A, pulled a thumb out of that hole.
a, the a - buse is all you crave.
a, when it's with you I'll be glad,

Cmaj9

Give me in - gre - di - ents, I'll mix it.
Sure you know just what is in store.
that I was right there just to show you,

D   Cmaj9   *Play 3 times*

How can you move with - out a goal?
Wait and see if I'll be - have.
at least it's more than what you have.

End Riff A

Guitar Solo

Gtr. 1: w/ Riff A (till fade)

Gadd4/B   G/B   A7sus4   Cmaj9

There real - ly nev - er is a good

111

Gadd4/B G/B A7sus4 Cmaj9 Gadd4/B G/B A7sus4 Cmaj9
time.
Gtr. 2 (dist.)
Gadd4/B G/B A7sus4 Cmaj9
Gtr. 2
D Cmaj9
Gtr. 3 (dist.)
steady gliss.
Gtr. 2 tacet
D Cmaj9
Gtr. 3

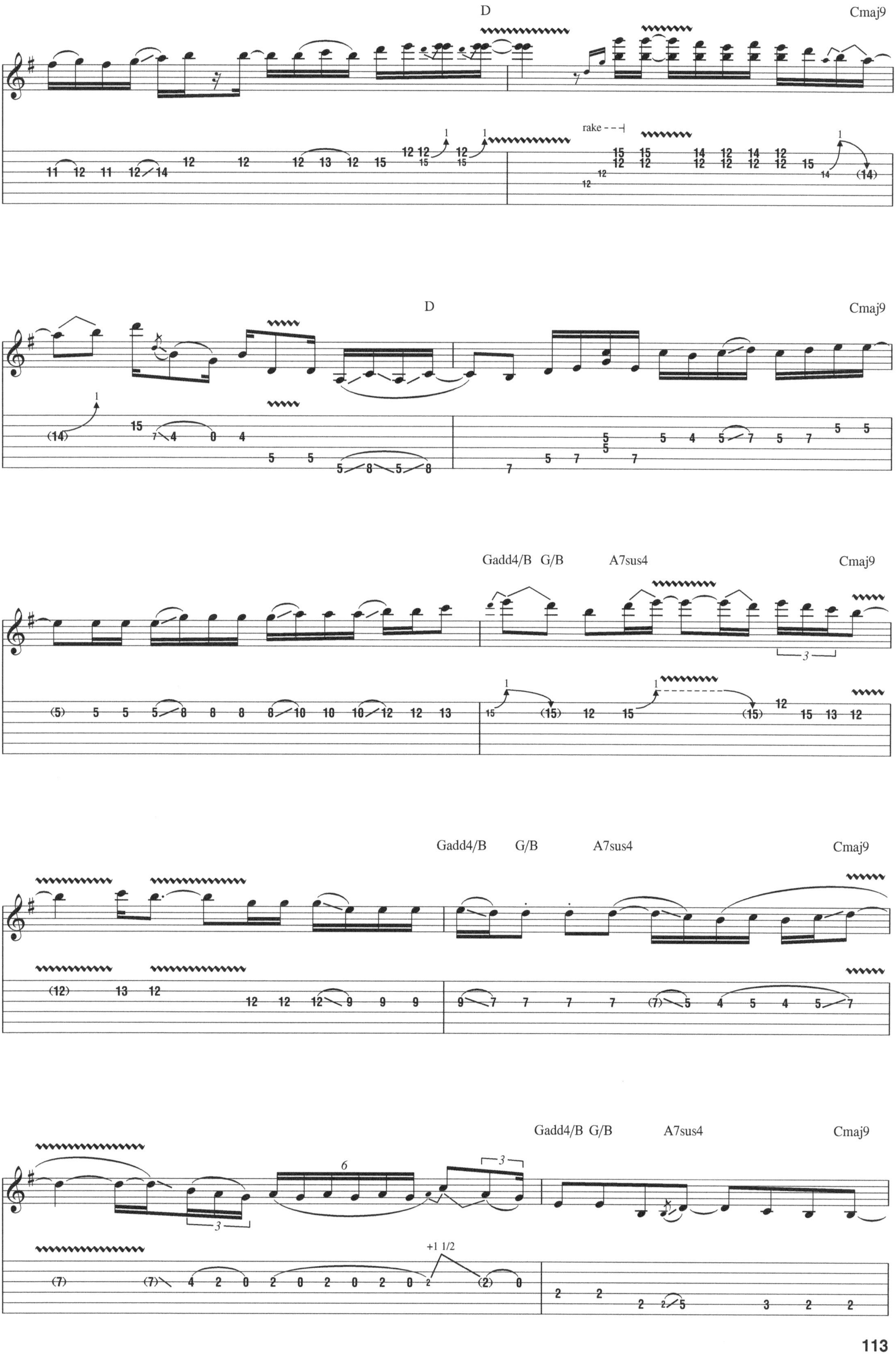
D
Cmaj9
rake
D
Cmaj9
Gadd4/B G/B
A7sus4
Cmaj9
Gadd4/B
G/B
A7sus4
Cmaj9
Gadd4/B G/B
A7sus4
Cmaj9
+1 1/2

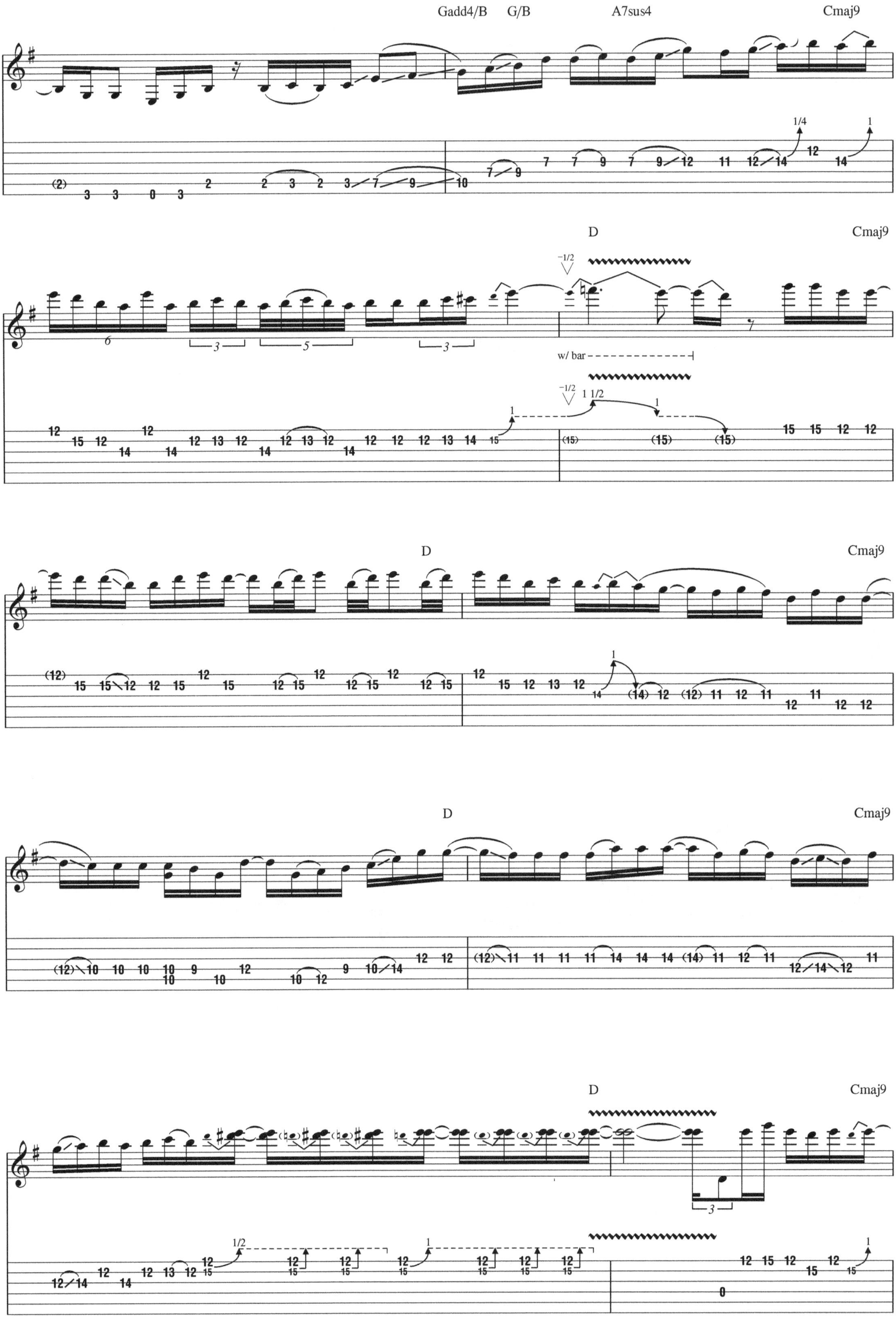
Gadd4/B
G/B
A7sus4
Cmaj9
D
Cmaj9
w/ bar
D
Cmaj9
D
Cmaj9
D
Cmaj9

Begin fade
Gadd4/B G/B A7sus4 Cmaj9
Gadd4/B G/B A7sus4 Cmaj9
let ring
Gadd4/B G/B A7sus4 Cmaj9
Fade out
Gadd4/B G/B A7sus4 Cmaj9
w/ bar

from *Green Mind*

The Wagon

Words and Music by J Mascis

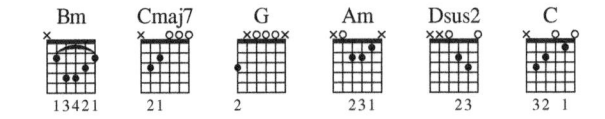

Bm   Cmaj7   G   Am   Dsus2   C

Verse
Fast ♩ = 177

Cadd9

1. A, there's a way I feel right now, wish you'd help me, don't know

Rhy. Fig. 1
Gtr. 1 (elec. sitar)
mf
w/ clean tone
let ring throughout

Gtr. 2 (elec.)
mf
w/ dist.
let ring

Gtr. 3 (acous.)
mf
let ring

Copyright © 1991 Spam As The Bread Music
All Rights Administered by Chrysalis Songs
All Rights Reserved   Used by Permission

how.

A, we're all nuts ___ so who ___ helps who, some help when no ___ one's got ___ a clue.

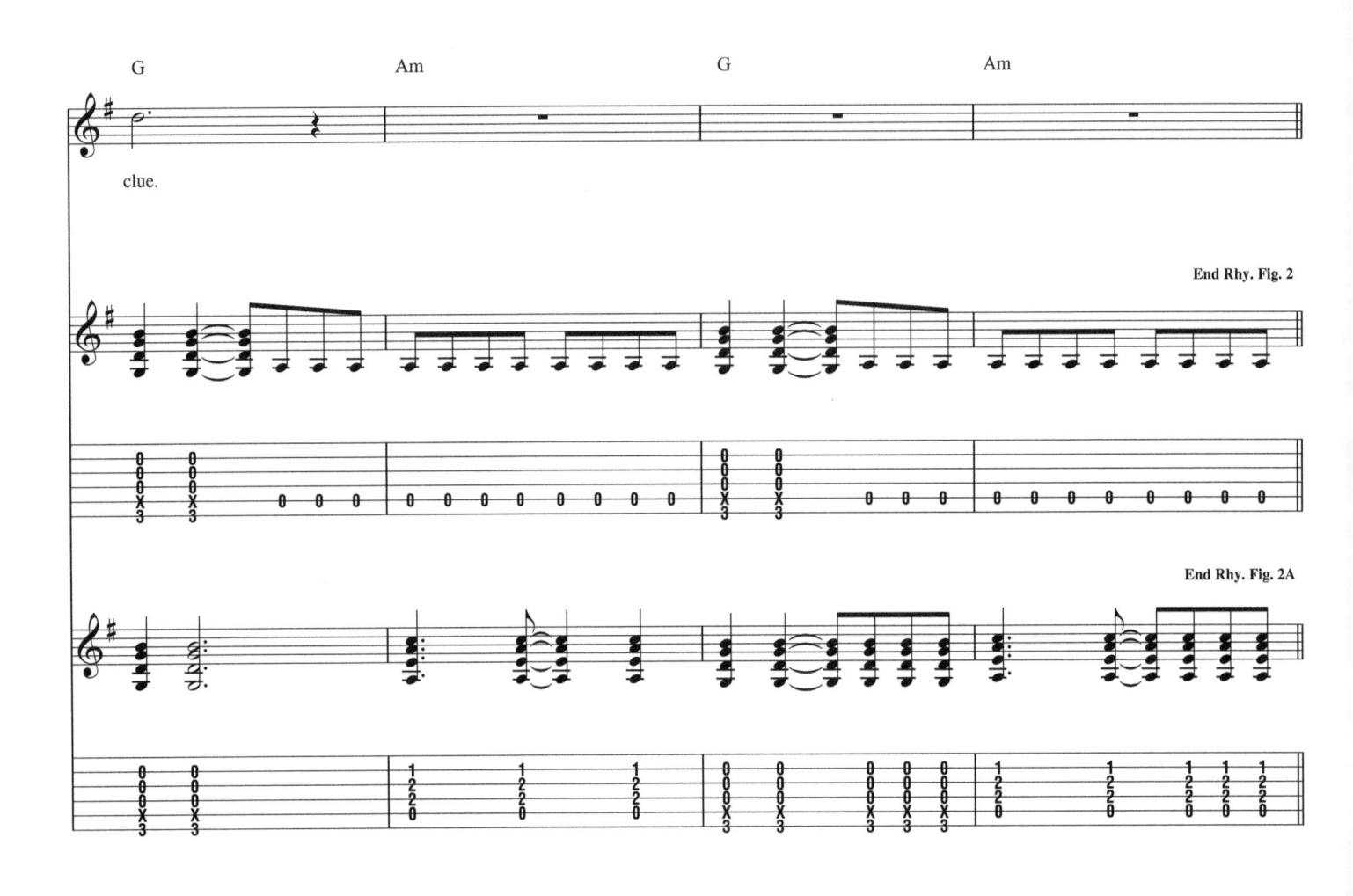

Pre-Chorus

Ba - by, why don't we? A, ba - by, why don't we?

Verse

Gtr. 1: w/ Rhy. Fig. 1 (2 times)
Gtrs. 2 & 3: w/ Rhy. Figs. 2 & 2A (2 times)
2nd time, Gtr. 5 tacet

2., 3. A, there's a place I'd like to go, when you get there then I'll know.

A, there's a place I know you've been, here's a wag-on, get on it.

Pre-Chorus

Gtr. 1: w/ Rhy. Fig. 3 (1st 4 meas.)
Gtrs. 2 & 3: w/ Rhy. Fig. 3A (1st 6 meas.)

Ba-by, why don't we? Ba-by, why don't we?

119

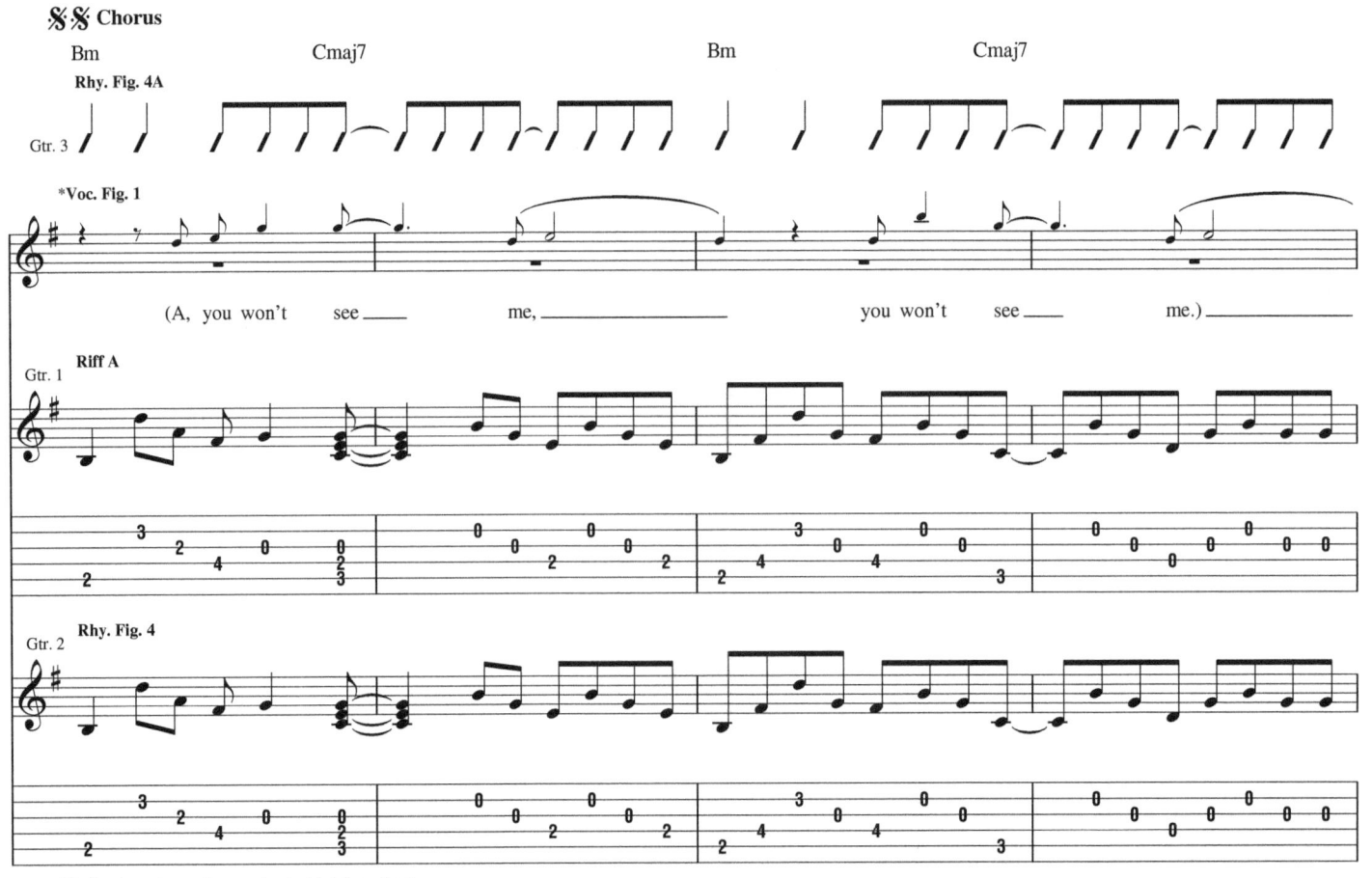

Chorus

Lyrics:
A, ba-by, why don't we? A, ba-by, why don't we? Why don't we?

(A, you won't see me, you won't see me.)

A, there you are and here I stand, tryin' to make you feel my hand. (A, you won't see me, you won't see me.)

I ring the doorbell in your mind, but it's locked from the outside. (A, you won't see me, you won't see me.)

A, you don't live there anyway, but I knock on it all

To Coda 2
Bm
Cmaj7
Bm
Cmaj7
day.
(You won't see me, you won't see me.)
Bridge
Dsus2
Bm
Rhy. Fig. 5A
Gtr. 3
A, there's a place I go but you're not there and I'm
Gtr. 4 (dist.)
f
Gtr. 2
Rhy. Fig. 5
let ring
let ring
*Voc. doubled, next 17 meas.
Gtrs. 2 & 3: w/ Rhy. Figs. 5 & 5A (3 times)
C
Dsus2
End Rhy. Fig. 5A
sup - posed to know how to get to where you're gon -
End Rhy. Fig. 5
let ring

Bm
C
Dsus2
- na be but you don't e - ven know.
So I'm flak -
Gtr. 4
hold bend
Bm
C
Dsus2
- ing while you're shak - ing it with ev - 'ry stone you fly.
With - out a mind,
hold
1 bend
Bm
C
with - out a spine,
what is it that you wan - na find?
Gtr. 4
1/2 hold bend
Gtr. 5 (dist.)
f
steady gliss.

Guitar Solo

Gtr. 1: w/ Riff A (last 4 meas.)
Gtrs. 2 & 3: w/ Rhy. Figs. 4 & 4A (last 4 meas.)
Gtr. 4 tacet
G
Am
G
Am
Gtr. 5
Bkgd. Voc.: w/ Voc. Fig. 1
Gtr. 1: w/ Riff A (2 1/2 times)
Gtrs. 2 & 3: w/ Rhy. Figs. 4 & 4A (2 1/2 times)
Bm
Cmaj7
Bm
Cmaj7
let ring
G
Am
G
Am
Bkgd. Voc.: w/ Voc. Fig. 1
Bm
Cmaj7
Bm
Cmaj7
G
Am
G
Am

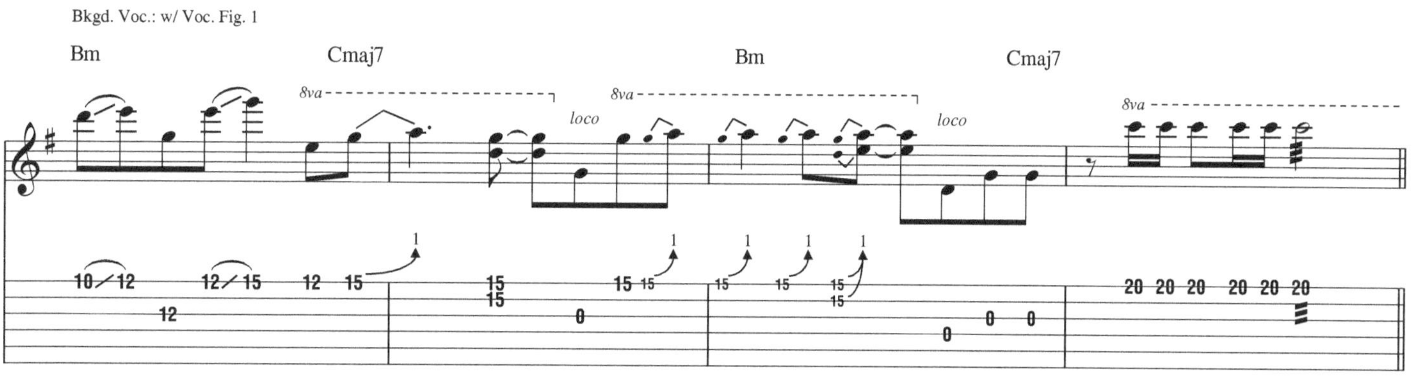
Bkgd. Voc.: w/ Voc. Fig. 1
Bm
Cmaj7
Bm
Cmaj7
8va
loco
8va
loco
8va

Bridge

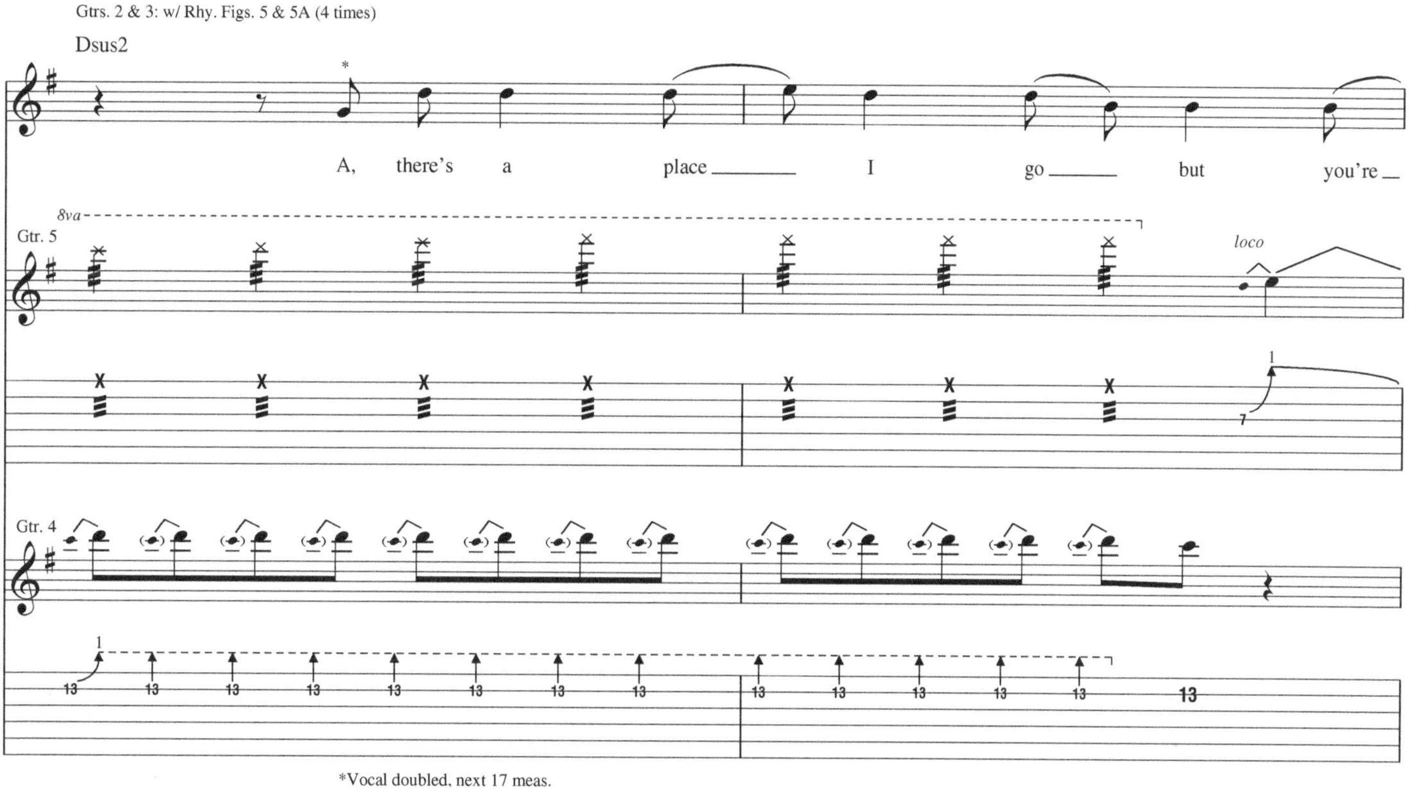
Gtrs. 2 & 3: w/ Rhy. Figs. 5 & 5A (4 times)
Dsus2
A, there's a place I go but you're
8va
Gtr. 5
loco
Gtr. 4
*Vocal doubled, next 17 meas.

Bm
C
Dsus2
not there and I'm sup - posed to know how to get

Bm
C
to where you're gon - na be but you don't e - ven know.
1/2

Dsus2
Bm
So I'm flail - ing while you're sail - ing off with - out
8va
loco

127

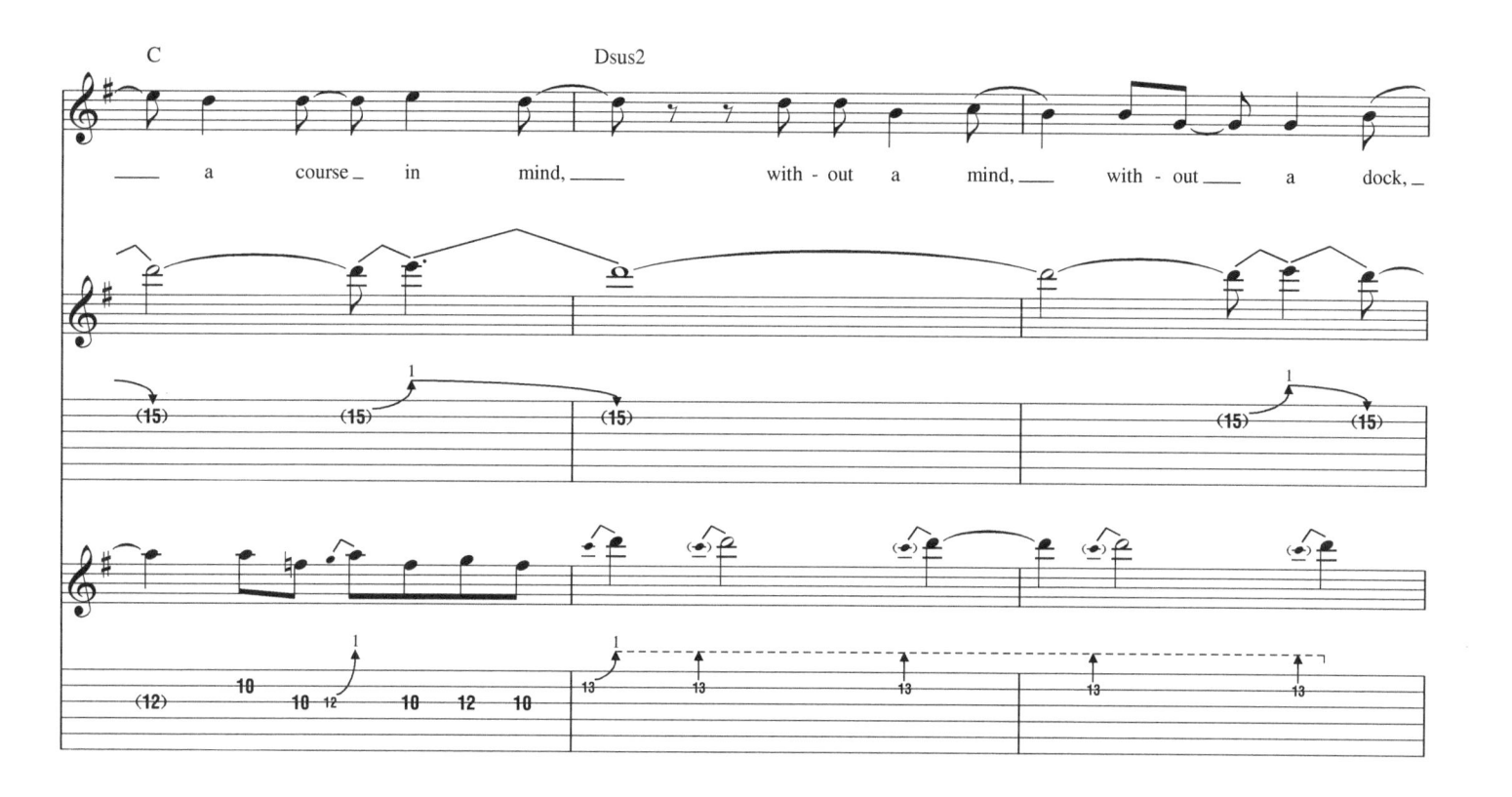

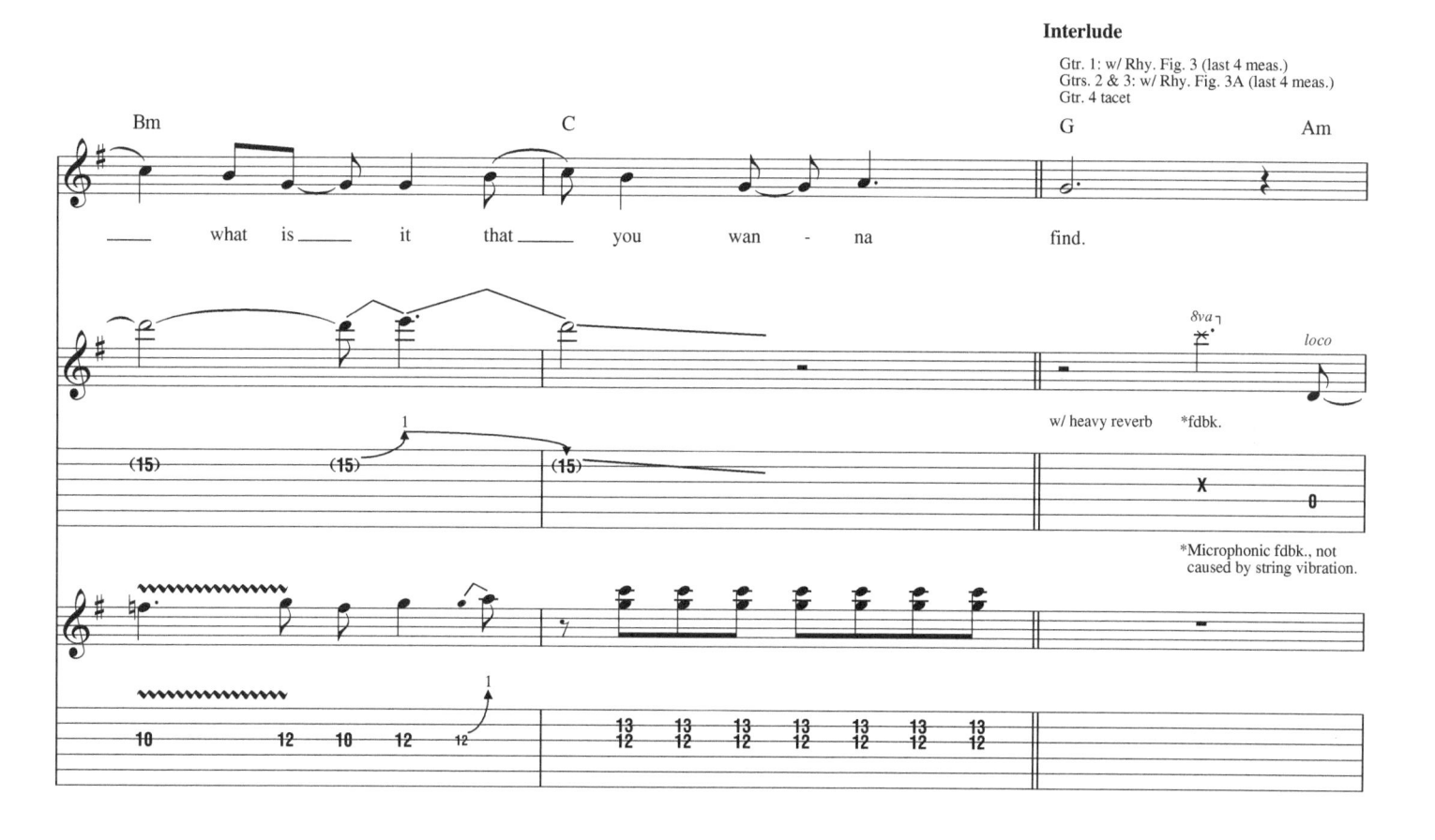

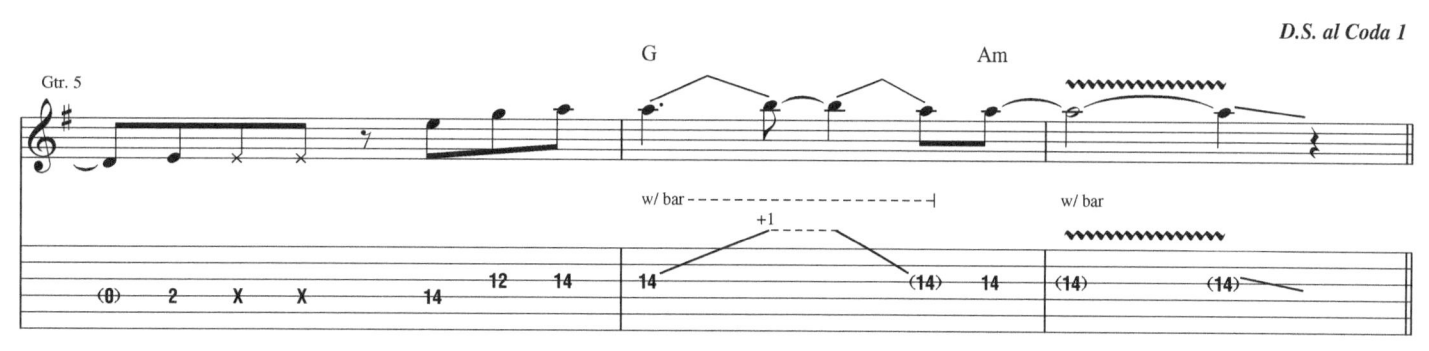

Coda 1

Pre-Chorus

Gtr. 1: w/ Rhy. Fig. 3
Gtrs. 2 & 3: w/ Rhy. Fig. 3A

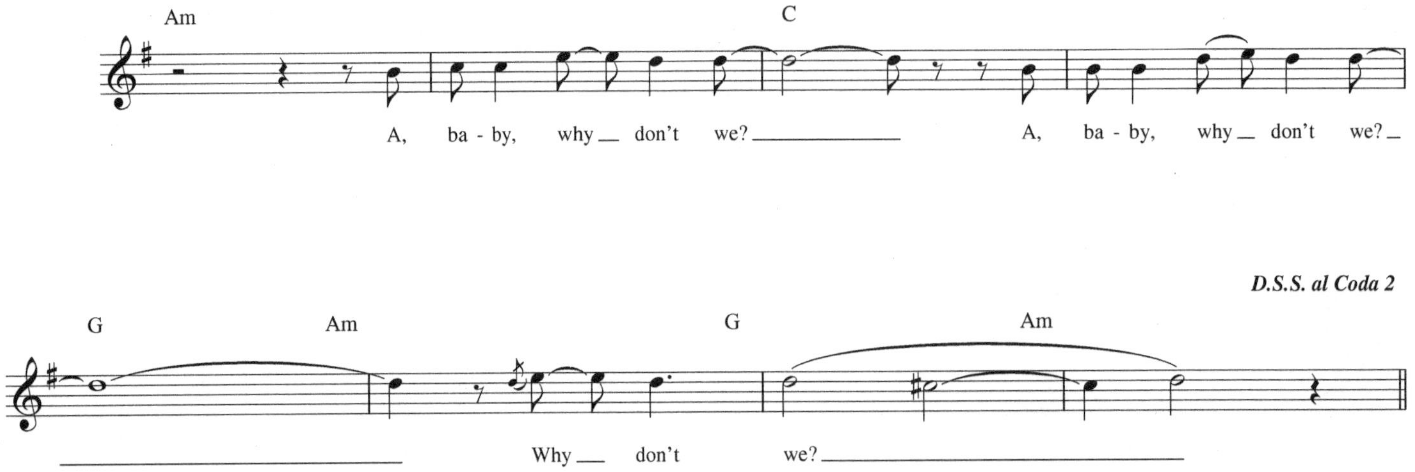

Coda 2

Outro

Free time

w/ misc. sound effects

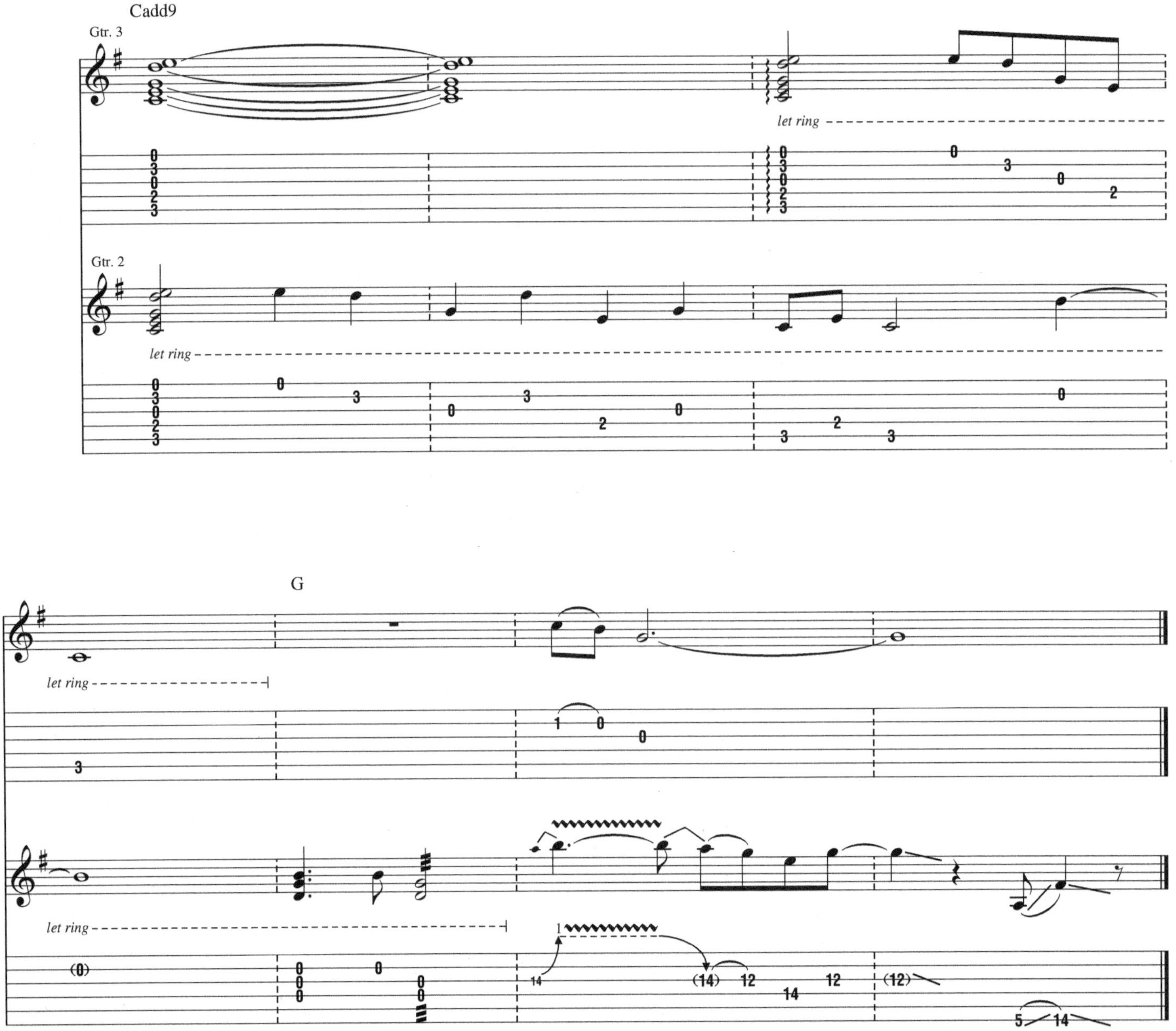